AF317040

ADVANCE PRAISE

In *Dutch Defense*, Johanna Kinney gives readers a great gift: a world of historical fiction enriched by her own knowledge and dramatic lived experience. Her characters leap from the page, animated by firsthand terror, suffering and tremendous courage. Whether we grew up hearing stories about World War II or we learned the facts in school, Kinney makes us feel deeply what the Dutch endured at the hands of the Nazis in a way that snippets of stories and history books cannot. That is the power of fiction: to enable us to viscerally imagine another's struggles. *Dutch Defense* is a cautionary tale, for all time but particularly our own, about infinitely relatable people whose rights, and, in many cases, lives, were snatched away when they never saw it coming.

— Doreen Vanderstoop, Author of *Watershed* (Freehand Books 2020)

A riveting story from the beginning, Johanna Kinney's *Dutch Defense* is a must-read. The author entertains with compelling characters and an intense plot against the very real background of World War II in the Netherlands, accomplishing this feat from an insider's view based upon her recollections of living through the German occupation during her young adult days.

—Elaine Stock, Author of the Resilient Women of WWII Trilogy (Amsterdam Publishers 2022)

A thrilling page-turner set in the Netherlands during the final year of WWII, *Dutch Defense* is a richly detailed semi-fictional account by Johanna Kinney. This novel is full of lively escapades that will hold readers spellbound from its first terrifying opening scene until its dramatic climax. *Dutch Defense* should be on the shelf of every person hoping to gain greater insight into the struggle to survive in the German-occupied Netherlands during the final year of WWII. I strongly recommend Johanna Kinney's *Dutch Defense*. It offers an abundance of insight and inspiration to all who delve into its pages.

—Peggy Anne McLeese, author of *The Magic Seven* (Xlibris)

Kinney's book *Dutch Defense* is a memoir of the heart and soul of Holland, its people, and her family during the German occupation 1940-1945. Kinney's storytelling ability and well-developed characters, together with her perspectives into the themes of loyalty, betrayal, consequences of choices, and forgiveness, make this book a must-read for reflective readers and discussion groups.

—Marjorie J. Hinds, Ph.D., retired school principal and researcher

Dutch Defense is a thoroughly satisfying read even without its historical context. The characters are clearly drawn and readily identifiable. The episodic nature of the narrative creates a rapid pace at the same time as it allows the reader to delve into the impact each incident has on the people involved. When one views the story in its historical context the impact of resistance to an invading army is put into very human terms. The courage, wisdom, sacrifice, and defiance of ordinary young men and women is what we take away from this novel even as its pages close with a hope for the future.

—Jan Boogerd, retired Chair and Professor at Algonquin College

DUTCH DEFENSE

A TRUE STORY OF STRUGGLE AND SURVIVAL DURING WORLD WAR II

JOHANNA KINNEY

ISBN 9789493322097 (ebook)

ISBN 9789493322073 (paperback)

ISBN 9789493322080 (hardcover)

Publisher: Amsterdam Publishers, The Netherlands

info@amsterdampublishers.com

Dutch Defense is part of the series WW2 Historical Fiction

Copyright © Johanna Kinney, 2023

All Rights Reserved. No part of this publication may be reproduced or transmitted in any form or by any means, electronic or mechanical, including photocopy, recording or any other information storage and retrieval system, without prior permission in writing from the publisher.

CONTENTS

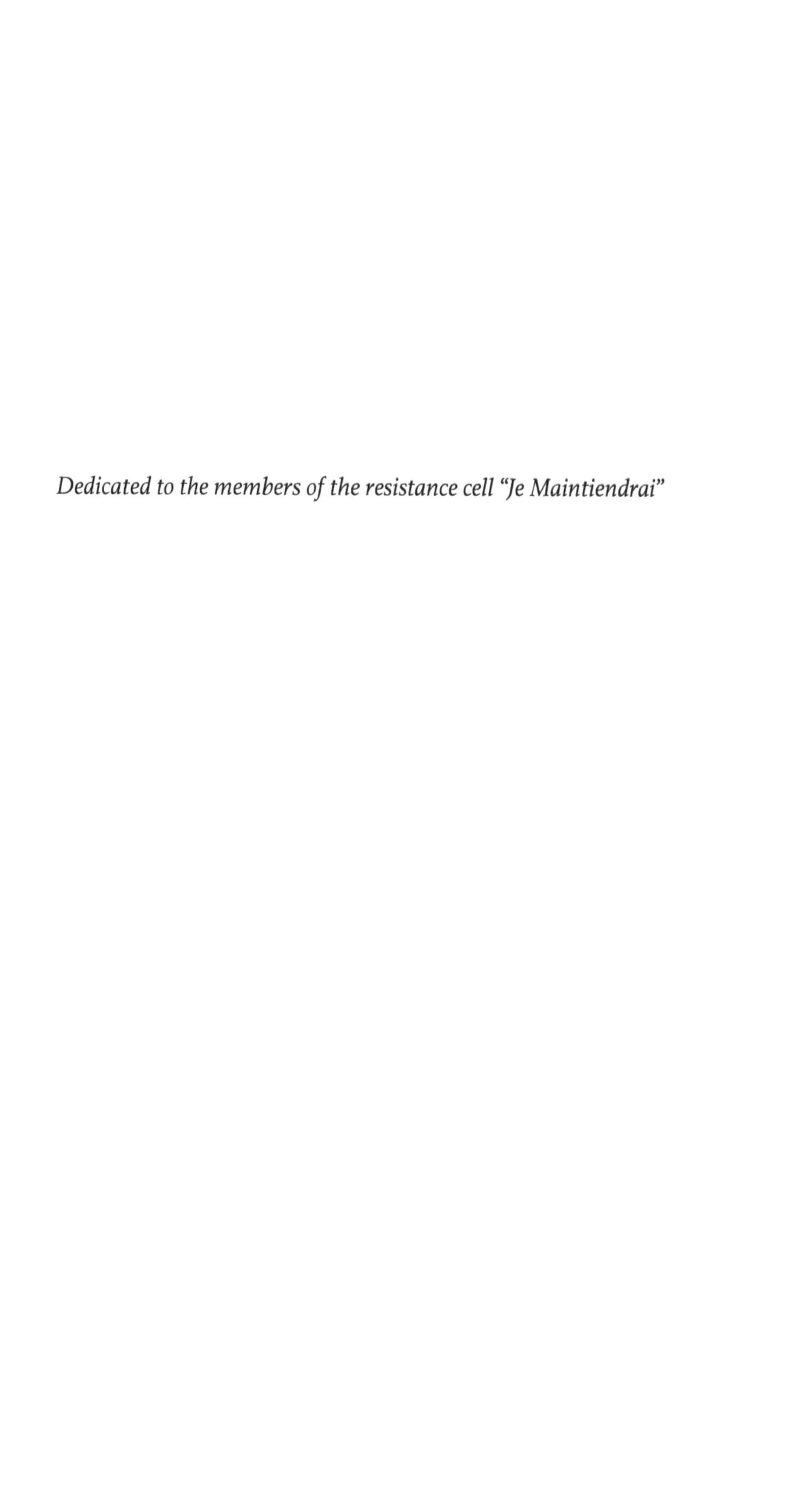

Dedicated to the members of the resistance cell "Je Maintiendrai"

PREFACE

This historical fiction story is based on my memories of the last year of the German occupation of the northwestern Netherlands during World War II. When the European war ended on May 4, 1945, German soldiers were still in town; we were waiting for the Allied forces to arrive.

"Je Maintiendrai," the motto of the Dutch royal family, was the name chosen by my brother and his friends for their resistance group, which was formed after the student strike in 1941. They received supplies through Allied airdrops. Most of the members did not survive the war.

With the German invasion in May 1940, all media were shut down. Even radios were confiscated. The Internet did not exist yet. No reporters were flying in to document what was happening. We were cut off from the outside world. News was shared by word of mouth and eventually by underground newspapers and "illegal" radios.

In this novel, I describe real actions and real events I witnessed, experienced, or was told about by reliable witnesses. Rumors circulated at that time. One such rumor was about a lawyer in The Hague who had access to the notorious prison in Scheveningen where political prisoners were held. I used his character and that of the local German *Kommandant* to build a storyline. As personalities, both are entirely fictional.

A word about the role of girl couriers during the last year of the war: In 1944, when the occupying Germans began to round up all men in the Netherlands between the ages of 18 and 45 and transport them to Germany (supposedly as laborers in weapons factories), men had to go underground to avoid this fate. The role of women changed. Their relative freedom to move about became essential, not only to the resistance, of course, but also to life itself.

I have avoided the word "Nazis" as a descriptor of the World War II occupying German army in the Netherlands to reflect that the word was not used to describe them during that time, as far as I know. The political fanaticism of the leaders and special forces of the Wehrmacht was only too well known, although the extent of fanaticism among regular army troops is uncertain. *Nationalsozialist* or not, they "followed orders."

Although the characters in this story were inspired by real people, they, and their relationships, are all fictional.

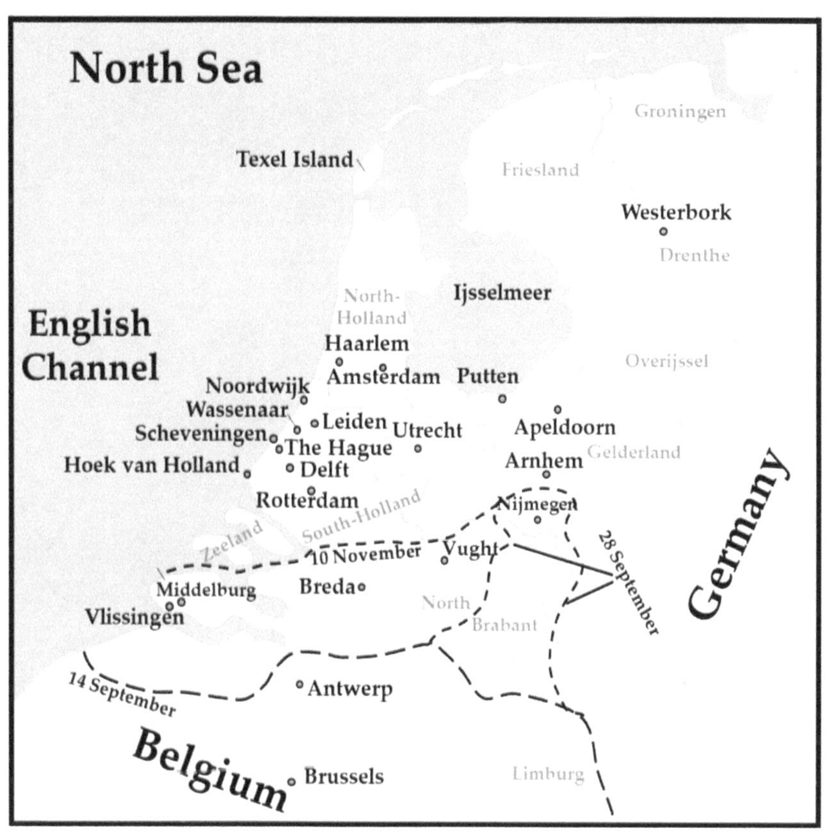

North Sea
Groningen
Texel Island
Friesland
Westerbork
Drenthe
English
Channel
North-
Holland
Ijsselmeer
Overijssel
Haarlem
Amsterdam
Putten
Noordwijk
Apeldoorn
Wassenaar
Leiden
Utrecht
Gelderland
Scheveningen
The Hague
Arnhem
Hoek van Holland
Delft
Rotterdam
South-Holland
Nijmegen
Germany
Zeeland
10 November
Vught
28 September
Middelburg
Breda
North
Vlissingen
Brabant
14 September
Antwerp
Limburg
Belgium
Brussels

THE STORY'S CHARACTERS AS THEY APPEAR

Anton and Leo: young men; members of the resistance

Alex van Vechtelen: lawyer; married to Nettie, with children Pieter and Karin

Gunther Blechmann: Waffen-SS *Ortskommandant* (local commander)

Marlise: young woman serving as a courier in the resistance

Barthold (Marlise's fiancé), Hugo, Steven, and Philip: members of the same resistance cell

Hugh ("Johnnie"): downed RAF pilot hiding from the Germans

Ada van Vechtelen: Alex's aunt

Henk and Marian van Waarden: he a doctor and she a pharmacist; supporters of the resistance

Riena: young woman serving as a courier in the resistance

Lottic: Anton's girlfriend and supporter of the resistance

Greta: supporter of the resistance, providing them shelter

Thea: Steven's fiancée

1

The radio announced, "Here is London." A few bars of the national anthem, then: "This is Radio Oranje." They huddled closer, listening for coded messages in the broadcast. At that moment, the doorbell rang.

With a deft movement, Anton placed the radio back in the hollow base of the coffee table. Alex handed him the glass top. They heard banging on the outside door—a shouting of "*Aufmachen!*" [Open up!] There was no time to put the screws back in. Alex carefully placed the chessboard exactly in the center of the tabletop, under the light. In the shadows against the wall he saw Leo, revolver in hand.

Alex pushed him out into the hallway. "Are you crazy? You know what to do! I'll try to keep them as long as I can!"

Making as much noise as possible, Alex followed the narrow beam of light from his pocket flashlight downstairs to the front door, all the while listening for the sounds of the two upstairs—had they had time to get to the double floor in the closet?

He clenched his fists. Damn Leo with that gun out. He'd have to throw him out. Leo had no right to jeopardize everybody. Fervently hoping that it was just a routine warning because of light leaking out of the house somewhere, he opened the door. A young helmeted soldier with a rifle over his shoulder stood on the doorstep.

"*Doktor* von Vechtelen?" he shouted, with the German pronunciation of Alex's last name and the German desire for formality.

"*Van* Vechtelen, yes," corrected Alex, as pleasantly as he could, covering the flashlight with his hand. "*Was ist los?*" [What's up?]

The soldier turned to a car parked near the curb and gave a nod.

In the almost total darkness of a new moon, Alex had trouble distinguishing the vehicle, his brain feverishly alert—no, it's not a Gestapo police van, it's what the top brass uses, complete with chauffeur... What on earth? Are they picking me up in that?

Then an officer alighted and walked stiffly into the front hall. The young soldier seemed to sense Alex's puzzlement, for he shouted before he turned to go back outside, "The Waffen-SS is taking possession of your house!"

Speechless for a moment, trying to assemble his thoughts, Alex faced the German officer.

With a slight bow, the German clicked his heels together. "*Kommandant* Gunther Blechmann!" Then, looking around appreciatively he said, "Beautiful staircase! How I love these old patrician Dutch houses! I have just come from admiring the gentlemen's homes on the canals in Amsterdam!"

Alex stared at him, an apparition from a nightmare. Then, drawing on his courtroom training for composure, he found somewhere in his mind the words for polite small talk of a lost time.

"Oh no, these houses are not as old as that—merely from the end of the last century. I have a little office here in the front. Yes, there is a dining room in the back, and the kitchen of course is a floor below." He spoke loudly, in German, keeping his tone jovial.

But the *Kommandant* motioned upstairs; he wanted to see bedrooms and bathrooms. With the flashlight, Alex led him into the bathroom, to the separate toilet, and then to his study, where the lamp cast a circle of light on the table.

The German stopped beside the table. "Ah, you play chess! I belonged to a chess club in my student years! This is an interesting game—your partner is not here?"

"I play from time to time with my niece, but of course she had to leave because of the curfew. We may be able to finish tomorrow perhaps?"

"But of course. I will not turn you out. I need a couple of rooms for me and a little room for my driver. Perhaps you and I may play a game now and then, *Herr Advokat*! I will arrange for my things and move in early in the morning." Picking up a rook, the *Kommandant* weighed it in the palm of his hand. "Beautiful craftsmanship—made of teakwood in the Far East. You must be a connoisseur."

Alex was lightheaded with relief. "But of course, we will play," he promised, keeping his tone friendly.

Leaning against the wall after seeing out the *Kommandant*, Alex breathed deeply, shutting his eyes for a brief moment. Then he bounded up two floors, ran into the back bedroom, opened the closet, and lifted a few floorboards, making sure to call out first, "Hey, it's me!"

Two handguns pointed directly at Alex. The pallid faces of Anton and Leo looked up from the narrow crawl space.

"For God's sake, put those guns away. What do you think this is, cowboys and Indians?" Alex fumbled for words, shaking with anger. As a lawyer, he had a legitimate dislike for firearms. He took pride in his reputation as a negotiator, preferring to wage war intellectually.

In the study, Anton and Leo huddled around the filing cabinet, from which Alex retrieved a few scraps of paper hidden in clients' files. From one of these, he decoded a telephone number.

A woman's voice answered Alex's first call. "You want to order something?"

"I have two tickets," he replied. "I'll send them over as soon as possible." He turned to Anton and Leo, scribbling on a notepad. "Here, find this address. Get them to open the door with the password. You can get there through a back alley from my house— only two street crossings and then a bicycle path hidden by shrubs. Memorize the address and get out now. I'll drop in within a week or so to bring you your things, or I'll send somebody."

Tearing up the paper with the address, Alex looked at the chessboard. "The *Kommandant* likes chess." He smiled at the two young faces. "And he really likes your play, Leo. He'll probably finish it for you."

Alex's hand that held the flashlight was still trembling when he let Anton and Leo out through the back door. He listened for the sound of the latch on the gate in the tall wooden fence. Then, all was quiet.

After a few minutes, Alex made his way over the slippery path, back to the faint outline of the kitchen door. The laburnum Nettie had planted too close to the house showered him with drops. Inside, he rubbed his head with the kitchen towel. He felt a great need to tell Nettie about the unexpected visitor and what was going to happen to their house.

He began to remove the traces of the stay of his last two "illegals" and knew it would be impossible to sleep unless he at least had tried to reach Nettie. This time, the connection came through quickly. He heard the ringing and then, thank God, the comforting sound of his father-in-law's voice: "I'll get her. Nettie! Nettie!"

They did not waste time on the phone. A long-distance call made them panicky. Alex suspected it was their ingrained fear of spending money, as if all their money would do them any good now.

Finally, the voice of Nettie, a little out of breath: "How are you? Is everything all right?"

"I am fine. The house has been requisitioned." He heard her gasp. "No, only part of it. I can stay. Everything's cleaned up. Don't you worry." Alex heard voices in the background and could picture Nettie's face in shock. Now he was on familiar terrain, calming her. "Really, it will be difficult, but I can manage. How are the children?"

Nettie's voice, though fainter now, was determined. "Pieter is really happy here with all the animals around and follows his grandfather everywhere. Karin doesn't like the school because she misses her friends. A difficult age, you know. She misses you. We all miss you. I worry so, Alex." The connection was broken.

Alex sat on his bed, a blanket pulled around his shoulders. There was a familiar ache in his chest. Their first separation, after 14 years of marriage—for how long? It was best not to think about it. But the images refused to obey.

Nettie. He could see her, answering the telephone. There was so much restraint in her, even in her appearance. The direct gaze of her golden-flecked, gray eyes under blonde lashes. The blunt cut of her dark-blonde hair and her pale-golden skin, resolutely free of creams and powder.

He loved that fine golden-hued skin all over her soft, rounded body. Uncovering that secret was what had first charmed and then captivated him in their university days. His friends didn't understand. Why this colorless, nondescript girl, when he was pursued by beautiful women? It had to be for her money.

Actually, Alex had been unaware of that aspect when he first met this quiet provincial girl. He'd been quite confident in his ability to make it on his own in the world, anyway. How much her family's financial status contributed to speeding up the wedding was another question.

He still enjoyed the company of pretty women, but in 14 years he hadn't been unfaithful once. His desire was entangled with the physical memory of Nettie's familiar smooth-skinned body.

Alex covered his face with his hands. Nettie's presence in his life had allowed him to become the man he was, satisfied in his work and his home life. This empty, dark house had been bustling with life's sounds and smells and the laughter of children.

The train station, last November. Pieter all excited at the prospect of the farm, his five-year-old mind unable to grasp his parents' mood. Nettie preoccupied, focused on the children, train schedules, luggage. Burned into Alex's mind was Karin's face, all twisted behind the window, tears streaming down her cheeks, her mouth forming the words, "Daddy, daddy!" The pain of the memory became such that Alex had to lean forward, hugging his chest.

Yet it was for the children that they had decided to give in to the urging of Alex's in-laws. But mainly for Karin, who had been such a bright little girl, and pretty too, with her father's blue eyes and thick dark hair. It had been a surprise to see his own features in his baby daughter's face. In the last year, he had seen her grow tall and thin and so pale. Twice she was sent home from school after a fainting spell. At least Karin and Pieter would be better fed on the farm and would maybe even be safer in the northeast of the country.

Alex turned off his reading lamp and stretched out in bed.

The room became a black nothingness with the heavy hangings in front of the windows. He felt too tired to get out of bed and roll them up. He shut his eyes and waited for sleep.

2

The town was silent in the darkness of the mild spring night. An almost imperceptible drizzle moistened the pavement. The only sound was scattered gunfire in the distance.

"Follow me," Anton whispered. "Remember? I have a cat's eyes."

He felt Leo step soundlessly close to his shoulder. City slickers were helpless on a night like this. As a farm boy, he'd had to learn how to find his way without the aid of city lights. There weren't many of those where he had grown up in a far eastern corner of the province of Overijssel. Tonight, the darkness of the new moon was like a cloak of safety.

Before crossing the street, Anton listened intently for the thuds of soldiers' boots on the pavement or the sounds of men talking. When all was quiet, he dashed across to the next alley, Leo in tow.

Alex's directions led to a path behind a row of houses. Here the problem was to find the open gate in the rough wooden fence. Anton's fear of encountering soldiers was now less strong than his worry about alerting the wrong people inside. There was no other way than to run their hands along the top of each fence. Anton felt sweat run down between his shoulder blades, or was it rain? Were they on the wrong track after all? What if there was another open gate?

Then he heard Leo mutter: "This is it."

A rickety gate gave way, and a brick path slick with rain led them to the dark outline of a house. Leo found an unlocked door and stumbled on the step up to it.

On a landing upstairs, voices could be heard behind a door, but they stopped abruptly when Anton knocked softly on it. After a silence, steps were audible on the other side.

A female voice asked, "Who is there?"

Leo and Anton provided the password simultaneously, and the door was slowly opened by a young woman with striking red hair. To Anton's relief, he recognized her as one of the couriers he had seen at Alex's house.

The small room was empty except for a table and chairs. A faint blue haze hung in the air. Anton sniffed. "Hm, real tobacco. So, when was the drop? Is that what you guys do with the English cigarettes? I thought they were meant for bribes. Interesting, don't you think, Leo?"

The redheaded woman opened a door in the back of the room. "It was not from a drop. We've got a British flier here—not for long, I hope. The guy finds it hard to keep quiet." She motioned to people in the next room. "Come in. It's okay. Meet these two; they are all right. I have seen them at Alex's place."

Three young men, probably in their early twenties, entered the room. One of them was so tall that he had to duck in the doorway.

"So, what happened?" the redhead asked.

"Alex has an SS *Kommandant* moving in early tomorrow morning," Anton replied.

"Jesus Christ! What next!"

Thunderstruck, they all fell silent.

Anton knew that Alex had functioned as one of their group's contacts, opening his home to meetings and providing a hiding place in an emergency. Alex knew his way around the jail where some of their friends were held. Since well before the war, his work as a lawyer had kept him in touch with prisoners. Somehow, he had managed to maintain his friendly relationship with several guards after the invasion. He was, in short, a much-needed contact. At times, he was able to tell them what actually had happened to their friends after their arrest.

The redhead was the first to speak, with a slight affectation in her voice. "Whatever this means, it adds to our own problems. Perhaps you can help us figure them out." She turned to Anton and Leo. "I am Marlise, and this is Barthold, my fiancé"—she gestured to a slender young man with thinning blond hair and glasses—"and the others will tell you who they are if they want to."

Of the other two young men who had entered the room, the shorter one smiled. His movements were quick and nervous, but his dark eyes were friendly. He ran his fingers through his straight dark hair. "As a matter of fact, I am Hugo, and this tall guy is my friend Steven. We were just discussing what to do with Johnnie, the RAF flier. He has been a royal pain. Tell them, Steven."

All faces turned to Steven, who took his time to answer. With one foot he pulled a chair toward him, turning it around. He sat down, a long leg stretched out on each side of the backrest, elbows leaning on it. When he spoke, it was with quiet directness. "The problem is, he doesn't realize how much harder things have become lately. He's had his own instructions in case he got downed, and he's trying to follow them. He treats us as if we owe him a return ticket. Besides, he doesn't seem to realize we hardly have any food to spare. The sooner we get rid of him, the better. But let's face it: it is getting harder to get them on the escape route to Portugal since the arrests in Belgium."

Hugo pulled out two chairs for the new arrivals, adding: "Steven has a lot of experience taking Allied fliers to the border, but we found out he is blacklisted now by the Gestapo. We all agreed he should lay low. If you have any ideas, feel free. But first, what are your names?"

Anton was self-conscious about his name, the same first name as Anton Mussert, the Dutch quisling. He tried to quickly think of a new one, but Leo spoiled the moment's opportunity by introducing them both. Resigned, Anton sat down with the others around the table. He was anxious to ask Steven for more details about possible escape routes. "With us here, too, you'll run out of food even faster. Perhaps we should leave with Johnnie when he goes. My friend Leo here is in the resistance and is Jewish. He's in double jeopardy, you might say."

All eyes turned to Leo.

Marlise broke the silence. "My job is to get you false identity papers and food coupons. Did you leave anything at Alex's?"

Hugo interrupted. "If anyone gets a chance to leave, it should be Steven. He has done his share, longer than anyone here. He has helped 19 British and American fliers across the border. His time is running out."

Steven gave a crooked smile. "Hey, we're all on the same level here. Anyway, getting out never was a picnic, and now it's nearly impossible. Before, I could still move around to escort guys to the border. One of my worst fears at the time was that they would say something in public, and some did, even on a crowded bus or train. They had no idea that they could blow the whole thing with one word of English. But now the Germans pick up any man between 18 and 45 for forced labor in Germany, at any time, any place."

Barthold hid a yawn behind his hand. "From what I have heard, Switzerland is a dead end, and so is Sweden. The escapees are put in camps and treated like delinquents."

"I think I know a solution," Anton volunteered. "Why don't we try to cross to England from Scheveningen, using a small rowboat on a dark night like this? We radio the British that we are bringing one of their own. It has been done before. I learned a lot in merchant marine school, and I know I can navigate. Who will go with me?" He looked around the table.

There was a long silence.

Suddenly Barthold jumped up. "The whole North Sea coast is one fortification of German bunkers. We cannot even get to the beach anymore. British patrol boats and German U-boats are ready to blow anything out of the water at the least suspicious sighting, and the North Sea is full of mines. Have you ever even tried to row a small boat across the North Sea? I was on the rowing team at Leiden University, but I wouldn't try it. I intend to survive this war, strange as it may seem." Standing behind Marlise's chair, he stroked her shoulders.

So far, Leo had listened quietly, but now he took them by surprise. "I'll go. What do I have to lose?"

Anton looked at his friend. He's all right, he thought. It was difficult to get to know Leo. He was smart, had finished law school young; he had these brooding silences, hiding what? Depths of knowledge Anton could only guess at.

"He's got enough common sense to listen to me when it's practical." Anton clapped Leo on the shoulder. "We're a team."

Marlise looked up at Barthold, smiling. "The solution is so obvious," she said. "The simplest way is that I go. We dress Johnnie up as a nun. He could pass as a woman, with that cute rosy face of his. That way, he'll keep his mouth shut en route. I escort him as far south as I can. I understand that friars and nuns usually help people across the border down there." She patted Barthold's hand before pushing his arms away. "I am going to give Philip a break while you think this over."

After Marlise had gone, Anton noticed that a stocky, somewhat older man had quietly entered and remained leaning against the wall, in the shadows.

Barthold followed Anton's gaze. "I thought you'd stay with our boy back there," he said to the man.

"No, he's sleeping," the other answered. "I thought I'd better check on what you kids are up to. So now you are going to send a woman out to do the dirty work? Why don't we just dump him somewhere? A spoiled brat from some private school, probably, who'll get us all in front of the firing squad without a tinge of remorse." He added in English, imitating a clipped Oxford accent, "We are not part of his old boys' club, you know."

Steven interfered. "I think Philip is right about one thing: it is a lousy idea to let a young girl like Marlise take this on. These guys can cause a lot of trouble, even the best of them. You have to make clear who's boss all the time."

Steven's set jaw and quiet air of authority left no doubt about the meaning of his words. "They don't have a clue as to what it means to live in an occupied country, where no stranger can be trusted. Americans at least seem to get into the spirit of a dangerous 'adventure,' as they see it. But some of the English! I remember one Brit who insisted he couldn't survive without his cup of tea in the morning, even though the smoke of the wood fire could give our hiding place away. I had to knock him out once. That stiff-upper-lip thing is highly overrated. Give me healthy fear, anytime."

Barthold leaned back, tilting his chair. He was cleanshaven and wore a threadbare jacket and tie, and only his pair of soiled tennis shoes gave away the concession to his present secret way of life. To Anton, Barthold's speech and bearing still had the unconscious arrogance of well-bred young men attending Leiden University.

"Of course I agree that Marlise shouldn't do it," Barthold said as he got up from the table, "but that doesn't mean I want to hear the suggestions of that communist over there. He is dangerous, I tell you. What do we know about him or what he is doing when he takes off alone at night? He'll get us into trouble before that RAF guy in the backroom. How can we trust him, anyway? He'd probably sell us all out to save his own hide and that of his commie friends."

Philip approached, a threatening, hulking figure, but Hugo intervened, placing himself between Barthold and Philip. "Don't be idiots! That's just what we need here, infighting. The Germans are our enemy, remember? Shut up, both of you. We have no time for this."

With a smile, Hugo looked at Anton and Leo. "Hey, we're not always like this, just most of the time. All the same, we must have food, with three more mouths to feed—Johnnie boy and now you two. Marlise will get more false identity cards for food stamps, but that may take a few days. We can only hope that Alex will help us out in the meantime. Come on, join us, Philip, to help solve our problem with Johnnie boy. You too, Barthold."

Barthold sat down, but Philip, with a sneer, left the room.

3

Alex paced back and forth in the small study, looking from time to time at the table with the chessboard. Was it riskier to leave the radio hidden in the table or to try to move it?

He glanced at the clock. For more than three years he had tuned in to the Radio Oranje broadcast at this time of the evening, feeling safe in his private retreat. How much would the *Kommandant* interfere in his life?

There was a knock on the door. Gunther Blechmann, the *Kommandant*, entered without waiting. "*Ich störe Sie nicht?*" [I'm not disturbing you?]

Alex felt his face burning. The gall of the man to just walk in after a perfunctory knock on the door! He cleared his throat. "Oh, I was preparing for a case, but please do come in and sit down."

Before Alex finished speaking, the German had already sat down at the table with the chessboard. "If I am distracting you, please say so; I will leave. But here we are, both lonely men. I hear that your wife and children have gone to Groningen?"

Alex started but recovered quickly. He nodded.

"You were worried about their safety here on the North Sea coast? But you know as well as I do, *mein Herr Advokat*, that any city can be a target for the Americans. It was a sad thing, the bombardment of Nijmegen in February."

There was a moment's silence. Then, slowly, Alex answered: "Yes, my family has gone to my in-laws' farm. The reason was, of course, that they will have more to eat there."

He would not be drawn into the German's line of questioning. The bombardment, which had resulted in the accidental killing of Dutch civilians, had been called a "navigational error" by the Allies, although the people of Nijmegen had wanted to believe it was done by the Luftwaffe to create resentment against the Allied forces.

But *Kommandant* Blechmann continued to commiserate. "Yes, a terrible thing, the destruction of that ancient Dutch city. And now the Americans are bombing our cities, night after night. We soldiers do not know if our families are safe. *Schreckliche Zeit.* My family is in Düsseldorf..."

Alex kept his eyes on the chess game. The truth was that the monotonous hum of the American bombers flying over at night filled him with hope that at last something was being done to end the tightening oppression of the occupation.

When he looked up, the German's eyes were brimming with tears, which filled Alex with a sudden rage. He abruptly stood up, turning his back on his visitor.

"I see your niece did not return yet," he heard the German say.

Dismayed, Alex turned around and noticed the German eyeing the chessboard.

"To finish the game, I mean, *Herr Advokat*. Were you playing black or white? White could end this game very quickly. Did I tell you that I played chess at university? We had excellent competitions between universities."

Alex took a deep breath. "I was playing black, and as I recall, it was my move, *Herr Kommandant*. If you wish, we can finish the game. My niece does not visit me every day, so I am sure she will forgive us."

The game was in its beginning stages, and the outcome was still unclear as far as Alex was concerned. Alex moved a pawn to free his bishop.

Gunther took a long time to consider each move, which allowed

Alex to observe his opponent more closely than he had done so far. Gunther was the typical German officer, stiffly erect and trim. A scar, perhaps from a *Mensur* (students' fencing duel) in his university days, ran across his right cheek. Behind steel-rimmed glasses, his pale-gray eyes protruded slightly. Thinning dusky-blond hair was smoothed to one side over his balding scalp.

The proximity of the illegal radio hidden under the chessboard had a peculiar effect on Alex's mind. It made him feel extraordinarily alert, as if his perceptions were sharpened. He sensed the inescapable logic of each move until Gunther made a fatal mistake. Alex glanced up to see if his opponent would reverse his move, but the German did not react.

In the few minutes he allowed himself to think, Alex weighed the importance of his next move. How good a player was Gunther? If he lost, would the veneer of good manners disappear? If Alex threw the game, would Gunther be aware of it, and how dangerous would his reaction be? Alex ultimately decided to play it straight.

Gunther quickly perceived the hopelessness of his position. "You have me, *Herr Advokat*," he said with a smile, "but how can a soldier win against a lawyer? Then again, I must be out of practice. Allow me to play again, but this time from the beginning. The night is still young."

He began to set up the black pieces. He stopped to examine the queen, holding the piece between his thumb and index finger, and said, "Do you mind if I ask you a lawyer's opinion about an incident? Last night, an SS officer walked alone along the canal. This morning his body was found in the water."

Alex looked up, a white pawn in his hand. "The last few nights were very dark," he said warily. "He must have taken a wrong turn..."

"*Ach*, one might think so. But you see, *mein lieber Herr Advokat*, the body was found without uniform, boots, or weapon. This was not an accident." Gunther pointed at his throat. "He was strangled before being thrown into the water."

Alex fought to remain outwardly calm. "A lawyer's opinion is usually not asked until a suspect is found." His voice sounded as if someone else had spoken.

Suddenly, the *Kommandant* jumped up, shouting, "Something must be done to stop those terrorists! The Dutch must be made to hate them, execrate them, and deliver them to us!"

Alex leaned back, watching him. His nervousness had disappeared; he had seen this kind of performance many times. The man in front of him acted like a wooden puppet, executing a mechanical trick. The German army trained them thoroughly, and screaming at those deemed inferior was a part of it.

The German sat down again. "Tonight, three prominent Dutch citizens will be arrested and brought to the jail in Scheveningen. They will be executed in front of your government buildings in 24 hours if the culprits do not give themselves up."

"Hostages!" Alex spat out. "You want my legal opinion?" But then he checked himself. "*Kommandant* Blechmann, you are a civilized, well-educated gentleman. Surely arresting and shooting innocent civilians goes against what you stand for. If anyone has the power to stop this, it is you, is it not? You have the responsibility."

The gray eyes looking back at him were expressionless. "Responsibility, yes, but power... There is always someone else to answer to. Anyway, it is too late."

"Too late? How will the perpetrators even know? We are not permitted to have radios!"

"Loudspeakers set up on street corners will announce the message. This type of news travels fast. But I will give some thought to your opinion, *Herr Advokat*. Especially since one of the hostages is a friend of yours and your family doctor, as I am told. But let us begin the game."

Alex, fired up from indignation and frustration, started the game with aggressive, offensive maneuvers. Yet he was calculating and alert to every move of his adversary, relying on his courtroom experience.

At first, the German admonished, "*Ach nein, Herr Advokat!* You are taking risks. You are too hasty!" But then he fell silent, pondering each move at length.

The game stretched into the early morning hours when the drone of high-flying bombers began. This time, the antiaircraft guns along the coast furiously rattled off multiple explosives.

Both men sat up, listening. Alex stood up and turned off the light before lifting the window covers. Beams of searchlights crossed in the dark sky. Along the coast, the *Luftabwehr* launched orange and green balls of fire into the night.

"There must be low-flying planes somewhere," he mumbled in Dutch.

Then, suddenly, a bright-orange glare lit up the city and the sky above.

"Flares," he said in English in the sudden quiet, for a moment forgetting the German standing beside him. When he remembered, he felt a delightful sense of triumph and thought, they are out there, and your time is almost up, *Kommandant*. If you are smart, you know it.

He realized that the *Kommandant* was watching his face intently in the orange light. Alex carefully rearranged the window covers and made his way to the table to turn on the light. "Perhaps we should call it a night. We'll finish the game tomorrow."

Gunther walked toward the door and paused on the doorstep. "I have given it some thought," he said. "I'll do this for you, *mein Herr Advokat*. After 24 hours we will free the hostages. In their place, we will execute three of the underground terrorists held in the jail." With a slight bow, he left.

Alex remained motionless in his chair, too drained to move. Finally, the chill of the unheated room drove him to his bedroom. In front of the French doors to the balcony, he spotted a small piece of paper on the floor. He let down the blackout covers and turned on the reading lamp beside the bed. He held the paper under the light and read: PLEASE HELP US—MARLISE.

4

Alex's night was restless. He tossed and turned in a bed that was unforgivingly hard on his thin frame. When sleep did come, troublesome dreams filled his mind with people, all wanting to talk to him with great urgency. When he answered, the sound of his own voice woke him to an empty room.

He then dreamed he was swimming but became caught in a slimy web, in which each movement could bring strangulation closer.

It was a relief to wake to the sound of birds singing outside.

Downstairs, he found his former housekeeper in the kitchen.

"Oh my goodness, Mr. van Vechtelen, you do look terrible! I heard about your new lodgers and thought you might need someone to help clean up around here. I brought you a couple of eggs from the farm and some real tea that someone saved from before the war." She lowered her voice and continued, "I also got you some fresh wheat bread. The old mill is still run on dark nights to get our wheat ground." She winked at him and unwrapped a coarse brown loaf. "You can have a real breakfast now. You look as if you need it."

Alex felt grateful, sitting down behind a plate with a slice of bread and a boiled egg, while the housekeeper came over with a steaming cup of tea. He recalled his habit of leaving his breakfast uneaten, slipping out the front door to avoid the housekeeper's morning chatter. Now the memory of those scorned meals haunted him.

He picked up his briefcase to go to his office, a 15-minute walk from his home. It was a cool morning, with a brisk wind whipping white clouds across the sky. A thin green veil hung over the trees. How exhilarating early spring mornings had been only a few years ago.

Crossing the street, he noticed a slight figure in a raincoat falling into step beside him. A green scarf tied under her chin hid her red hair, but Alex immediately recognized the profile of Marlise.

"Are you coming?" she asked. "I know you're angry about last night, but we are desperate."

He looked straight ahead. "Whose harebrained idea was that?"

"Steven climbed the drainpipe to your balcony. He is very athletic." She giggled. "Anyway, we have bad news that you should know."

Alex turned into the entrance to his building. "I'll be there at five." So far, he had avoided visiting any of the resistance groups in daylight, but with the curfew earlier and the days lengthening, he had no choice.

After work, feeling self-conscious, Alex attempted to walk nonchalantly among the five o'clock crowd. He kept the brim of his hat pulled low under the pretext of holding on to it in the wind.

He found himself in the narrow hallway and let out a sigh of relief. He knocked softly—three fast, two slow—and gave the password when asked. What nonsense, really, as if they would have any chance of escaping if the time came.

Marlise welcomed him in, but lost her composure at the sight of him. "Oh, Alex, they are fighting, and we are out of food. It makes them dangerously edgy, you know."

Alex put his arm around her. "You should go home to your parents. I mean it. Please consider it. I am begging you."

"No, I want to be with Barthold. To think that we would have been married by now if the war hadn't ruined everything. Who knows if we'll ever get to enjoy a married life together?"

"Just make sure you don't get pregnant," he blurted out. "This is not a time to have babies."

Marlise pulled away with a quizzical look in her eyes. "So I realize, but I haven't had a period in over a year now."

Alex started to form a response, but she continued, "Don't look so surprised. Have you talked to any young women lately? It's a lack of something in our terrific food rations."

Alex looked at her more closely. Her skin was very pale, with an almost transparent quality, and her eyes were deep-set and large. He took her hand, a small boyish hand with rough, short nails, and kissed it.

"Please, you have done enough. Go home. But first, make us some tea." He pulled the loaf and bag of tea leaves from his briefcase.

Marlise jumped up, clapping her hands. "Look at this! Real tea and bread! I'll be back in a minute!"

But Alex held her arm. "Listen to me. I'll help you—" He stopped abruptly.

The others walked in and assembled around the table as if it was a business meeting. Philip arrived last, finding a seat at the end of the table beside Marlise. Tension hung in the air.

When sliced bread and steaming tea were put in front of them, their faces brightened. Despite its rough, dry texture, the bread disappeared in a few minutes. The Englishman, seated between Hugo and Steven, joined eagerly.

Alex leaned across the table to address him in English. "We will do our utmost to get you back to England," he said in his most courteous manner. "In the meantime, things may be a bit rough."

The pilot's face lifted up to Alex, who at that moment was surprised by how young the Englishman looked, with a shock of reddish-blond hair and sparse red stubbles on his chin, eyes darkened in anger. "These blokes treat me like a prisoner in this bloody place! It's worse than being a prisoner of war, I say!"

Alex changed his tone slightly. "I assure you that all these people are prepared to risk their life for you. But you should know"—he spoke more sternly now—"that London has been informed that you are with us, and neither they nor we will risk our entire operation for you. And as far as your treatment goes, the SS tends to avoid taking prisoners these days, if you know what I mean."

"But if London knows, why hasn't the air force picked me up?"

"This is a small crowded country," Alex answered patiently. "The planes make drops, but they don't land here. They can do that in France, but here it's too risky."

"I'll remember to crash over France next time," the Englishman said, grinning.

Alex looked around the table at the others. "Before you tell me your news, I have to tell you something that troubles me. Three of our friends will be executed tomorrow, and I am at least in part responsible."

Marlise put her hand on his arm. "How can you be responsible?"

Alex took a deep breath and explained. "An SS officer was killed the night before last. The *Kommandant* ordered three hostages to be shot unless the killers gave themselves up today. I appealed to his honor as an officer and asked him to let the hostages go."

The others looked away.

"He said that as a favor to me, he would have three political prisoners shot instead."

"Who? Who will be shot?" Marlise asked.

"I did not ask, but I don't think he knew who. I was afraid to appear too interested in the fate of our friends."

Leo broke his silence. "We didn't learn this stuff in law school. What a messy dilemma, don't you think, Counselor?"

Marlise jumped up and banged her fist on the table. "That's all you have to say? What have we become? I hate it, absolutely hate it!"

Barthold walked over to her and gently coaxed her to sit down again. "Now, now, of course we care, but what can we do? We don't know who they are, and we don't have enough time."

Philip pushed away from the table, scraping his chair sharply over the wooden floor. "You are all amateurs," he said hoarsely. "This is no war for incompetent fools. There is no room for sentimentality. Alex was right in what he did, and damn lucky for everybody. Those three will not talk anymore. They are lucky too." Philip turned to Marlise, his jaw set and dark eyes blazing. "What do you think happens to them, eh, when the Gestapo suspects they know something?" He then looked at Alex. "Someone should attend to the receiver in the back room." Alex made no attempt to keep him from leaving.

Marlise said, "My God, his anger was palpable. He really hates me."

Barthold took Philip's seat. "You are just tense," he said to Marlise. "Perhaps it is time to tell Alex what happened to your contact."

Alex turned to her, but Hugo reached across the table to shake his hand and said, "To tell you the truth, Alex, you should be congratulated. Those three were candidates for death anyway, and then it's the sooner the better, as far as I'm concerned. I am telling you, I will not be caught alive. I'll shoot my way out and take one or two of them with me."

Steven murmured consent. "You did the right thing. Besides, your relationship with the *Kommandant* may be invaluable."

Marlise was still thin-lipped with anger. "I don't like what we are becoming. We are losing normal human feelings." She clasped her hands as if in prayer. "Anyway, I'll give you my bad news. I went to my contact's house. His wife was crying and told me he was arrested. The woman who worked in the registry office was also arrested."

Alex inhaled sharply. "Did he know your name, your location?"

"Just my first name. Definitely not our address. Their neighbors might have seen me occasionally."

Alex stood up. He tried to calm his nerves. "You can't go out for the next few days. I will find a new courier to bring supplies." He turned to the others. "We will get Marlise home to her parents as soon as possible." He ignored her gesture of protest. "We have to find out how far this is going because it could be very serious for everybody. London has to know about this new development. I'd better be going."

"There is something else," Steven said. The expression in his eyes stopped Alex in his tracks. "It's this guy Philip you sent us. He doesn't exactly fit in. He comes and goes and is secretive. Perhaps it's a good thing we don't know."

Alex collected his thoughts before responding. "Believe me, it's better to have Philip as a friend than as an enemy. He is on our side. Hopefully, it won't be for much longer." He looked at the faces around the table. "Remember, things are going badly for the Germans, even though we don't see that here. The Allied forces are in Italy, the Soviets have turned the tide in the East, and soon we will have an invasion somewhere on the west coast of Europe."

Steven nodded. "There are rumors of a plot by top German officers to get rid of Hitler. Something is bound to happen if we can only hang in long enough."

"It is April already," Anton said. "If it's going to happen this summer, what are they waiting for?" He nodded at Leo. "Anyway, Leo and I have a plan. We are going to cross the North Sea to England on a dark night. I know some fishermen in Scheveningen who will let us have a small boat. What do you say, Alex?"

Alex thought, it's a crazy plan, but perhaps no crazier than staying here. At this point, I have no idea what the future holds for us.

"So, what's your opinion?" Leo brought Alex back to the present. "I feel as if I'm in a trap, just waiting for it to spring. Anything must be better."

"If you go, plan it carefully for the safety of those left behind. The way I see it, things will get much worse here before they get better. But first I must find another safe place for you."

Instead of walking home, Alex ran alongside the streetcar rails. He caught up with one and jumped in. The old car lurched along on the tracks. The wind had died down. In the cool evening, the sun's golden rays slanted over roofs and flowering treetops. Birds were singing and chirping. But somehow Alex felt like a spectator, no longer connected to this world. He got off the streetcar in front of an old church and went inside. Behind the altar, Alex followed a few steps into a passage that led to a side door. This opened onto a narrow cobblestone street lined with ancient houses and shops. To the accompaniment of the tinkling door chime, he entered one that displayed antique books in a tiny window.

Inside, Alex walked through a narrow, low-ceilinged hallway to a back room, where an old printing press was clicking away.

A few men stood around, watching. "What brings you here?" one of them asked, stacking a bundle of roughly printed newsletters. "You want to take some of these off our hands? We now have kids delivering them. It's getting harder to find couriers stealthy enough to do this work without getting caught."

"That is why I came—to talk about the arrests. We must let them know in London."

"It's been done. We sent the message, but so far we haven't heard anything back."

5

Alex woke to the unusual smell of bacon frying. It startled him into action. He flicked on the gas water heater above the bathtub and washed himself, standing shivering in the tub. The hot stream clouded the cool room in steam. He dressed for the office as if for a normal day, but the smell was still there. Was it a hallucination?

Gunther's driver was in the kitchen, frying ham.

Alex stiffened. Where did they get it from when the stores were empty?

Alex's bicycle was in the shed; he rarely used it these days. Since his car had been requisitioned, he preferred to walk. A brown canvas double pannier hung across the rear bike rack. He strapped his briefcase in one side. His long raincoat had a split in the back. To avoid catching the bottom in the spokes, he turned up the flaps and buttoned them on each side.

Alex pumped up the soft, patchy tires cautiously, since they could easily blow. With his hat pushed down on his brow, he headed toward the southwest end of town. Despite his upright position on the bicycle, it was a challenge to maintain his dignity on the shaky ride. From time to time he let out a hearty oath at an unexpected bump.

It wasn't only the poorly maintained pavement since the invasion. The tires had been patched so many times since then that they were lumpy. "*Das Vaterland*" had a gargantuan hunger for any conceivable supplies. It had not taken long to realize what the "German hand extended to the Dutch, our Germanic brothers," meant in reality. The "privilege" of a German civilian administration had made their systematic plunder of the Netherlands extremely efficient.

Like others, Alex and Nettie had learned that in the first few days of the occupation. Nettie had put their address in a parcel on a truck collecting for the survivors of the bombardment of Rotterdam. A thank-you note arrived, months later, from a city in Germany. It was only the beginning. How naïve we were, he thought. As if we had any control left of anything! We still had to learn that the Aryan brother's hand was a fist squeezing the country dry.

In a neighborhood of brick sidewalks and low-level red brick apartment buildings, he gave up and walked the rest of the way.

A flight of concrete steps led to three front doors, one of which had a nameplate: "A. van Vechtelen."

"Hello!" he called, letting himself in. "Ada?"

The hallway was small but clean and well furnished. A Bible text in Gothic letters hung on the wall: "Blessed are the peacemakers, for they will be called the children of God."

A middle-aged woman came rushing to the door. "What's happened?" she whispered, brushing graying strands of hair back and repinning the knot on top of her head. "Good Lord, what's happened now?"

"I need this apartment," he said. "I mean, I need your apartment for a group of illegals, and I need it today."

She raised both hands in desperation. "I can't do it. When you brought the Jewish baby here, you told me that was the last. I just can't."

"Ada, listen. You know that I found relatives of the baby's non-Jewish grandmother who have agreed to hide her out in the country. I need you to go with the baby to take care of her. The best thing is to leave today because the boys will have to move in immediately."

He sat down with her, holding her hands. "Ada, it's a matter of life and death. This is not going to last forever. You are a true Christian, a woman of real faith; that's why I'm asking you. I often remind myself of how much you have done already."

Her blue eyes moistened and the color in her cheeks deepened. "What if they trace her relatives just as you have? They'd find her more easily there than here. I want to keep her as safe as I can."

"You are my favorite aunt, my father's baby sister. Do you think I want to endanger you more than I already have?" He kissed her on her smooth cheek. "That's why it is safer for you not to stay here with the group of illegals. Besides, I know you are too attached to the little girl to let her out of your sight."

She stood up, pressing a bundle of baby clothes to her chest. "You want to see her?"

But Alex continued. "This is a short-term solution—not longer than a couple of weeks. What is the alternative?" He looked at the windows. Good, high off the street. A good distance from the building across, with an almost blind wall. "How much can you trust your neighbors?" He nodded in the direction of the front door.

Ada let out a hearty, full-throated laugh. "Well, it seems to be a done deed. If you were not my favorite nephew... I just wish you were still with our church. I pray for you every day."

He put his arm around her shoulders. "I need your prayers more than ever." He sighed. "I am sending someone to take you to the train station in a few hours. Take nothing with you, just the baby. I'll try to send you some clothing later."

As they talked, they had gone into the baby's room. She was awake; curly brown hair framed a round face with large dark-blue eyes, and a still-toothless mouth smiled delightedly at the attention given her. Ada fussed and cooed, bending over to kiss the top of her head. The baby lay bare-bottomed on a red rubber mat with slits, a solution to the lack of diapers. She was dressed in a scrupulously clean white knitted sweater and socks.

"She looks great, Ada." Alex smiled back at the little face. "I don't know how you do it, with the soap rations so small."

Ada beamed with pride. "Remember, I am a nurse, retired or not. I boil her clothing, and I get some help with food from the church."

He knew she wanted to keep him there and talk, but he pleaded an urgent meeting at the office and left.

Back on the road, he thought warmly of Ada, who was probably praying or reading the Bible at her well-polished oak table, with the small Persian rug thrown over it. Ada may never see her beloved things again, yet she never mentioned it to him.

Oh, the petit bourgeois horror of his rebellious teenage years! How he had resented the narrow, stifling environment of his Calvinist upbringing—the daily Bible readings, the lengthy church sermons twice on Sundays. How liberated he had felt as soon as he had left home; never to look back, he was certain of it. And now these same people were truly heroic and dependable, highly principled, and fearless when arrested.

The truly devout Christians and the truly atheist communists have something in common, he thought. You can't live with them, but from what I hear they're great to face death with.

The morning was gray and still, with a low cloud cover. His thoughts shifted to the days when Nettie and he had their first baby. How he had enjoyed being a new father! He smiled at the memory of Karin toddling toward him with outstretched arms when he came home.

Suddenly, he heard the hum of airplane engines and the high-pitched whining of sirens—then, almost immediately after, so swift that the three sounds seemed to happen all at once, the boom of a single explosion.

Alex was sure it had come from the inner city ahead of him. He looked up at the leaden sky, waiting for a reaction. The planes got away, apparently. In the early years of the war, Messerschmitts would take off and engage in air battles, but they did not seem to be around anymore.

The few people in the streets, at first alarmed, were now shouting at each other. "What was that? Where was that?"

Alex picked up speed, struggling along on his bicycle. This did not seem to be a bomb gone astray. A *Panzerwagen* [armored car] rushed past him in the same direction. The closer he came to the center of the town, the more he noticed the commotion in the streets.

People clustered together, talking and gesticulating. German military rushed about.

He arrived at his office, and everybody was gathered around his secretary's desk. She looked up. "They bombed the registry office," she said, watching Alex's eyes with a peculiar look, "and from what I hear it was a perfect hit. The buildings beside it were untouched."

She had worked with Alex for as long as he had been with the firm, and she had been the senior partner's secretary before he retired. In her fifties now, she had become the unofficial manager of the firm and a motherly, supportive presence.

One of Alex's partners spoke up, visibly angry. "Exactly, it was an inside job if ever there was one! What are the Germans going to do? They won't take this lying down. We'll have to pay for it, I tell you."

Alex remained silent, but to his surprise, his secretary took over. "Maybe there won't be a retaliation. After all, the Dutch employees working there today didn't stand a chance, so I heard. A friend of mine said nothing was left but a pile of rubble." She kept looking at Alex as if to warn him about something and then slipped him a message scrawled on notepaper: A GERMAN SOLDIER IS IN YOUR OFFICE.

Alex looked at the calendar on her desk—April 11—and then at his appointment book. "Hm, I must have forgotten about this meeting. Excuse me."

His heart was pounding. He opened the door soundlessly and stepped into his office.

It was a second-floor corner office with large windows on both sides looking down over two busy city streets. A tall, thin figure in the familiar uniform of an SS officer stood beside the desk with his back to the door, looking out the window. Alex coughed, and the man turned around.

It was Barthold, his face ashen. He nodded at the door. Alex turned around to close it, then motioned Barthold to a chair. They faced each other across the desk.

"Marlise... she is... she was arrested today." The words seemed to hurt Barthold's throat.

The two men stared at each other, speechless.

Alex began to pace back and forth in the office, trying to control his anger. "Why? How? I told her not to go outside!"

Barthold finally said in a low, expressionless voice, "You also told her to go home to her family. She became convinced that it was safer for her to go, safer for all of us. Philip said she was no longer a help to us, that she had become a liability. After that, I was afraid she'd just take off, so I decided I'd take her to the station and get her on a train." He covered his face with his hands.

Alex gestured at the uniform, the shiny black boots. "Where did you get this?"

"Philip. He had the outfit and a black wig for Marlise. My German is good, so we made up a story. She would play the part of a cheap Dutch tart. Oh God, when I think… if only we would not have done that." He slumped in his seat.

Alex leaned over the desk. "Pull yourself together, Barthold. I need to hear the story. Tell me what happened from the beginning."

"She acted as if it was a game, laughing about the wig and the garish makeup on her face, you know. The contempt of the people in the tram bothered her a bit, but we were so believable. I took her to the Staatsspoor station and put her on the train home. When the train started to move, I was sure we had pulled it off."

He seemed unable to go on, but Alex shook his shoulder. "Hey, speak up, will you?"

"When I turned around, I saw all these Germans, swarms of them. They came up the stairs and cordoned off every exit. Soldiers with rifles boarded the trains, and none were permitted to leave. There was so much shouting."

Alex sat back down. It was important to keep a cool head. "An identity check, maybe. It could have been to round up men for labor in Germany. Didn't you say her train had left?"

"No, Jesus, man! Why would I come here then? Hell, they stopped her train at the end of the platform. I saw two soldiers take her off the train. She looked at me, but it was as if she wasn't seeing anything."

Alex interrupted. "It could be a routine check for Jews. She has an Aryan identity card. They'll have to let her go."

"The ID picture doesn't look much like her today, now, does it?"

Barthold's anger turned into his usual sarcasm. "You don't think they'll wonder why the disguise?"

Alex suppressed his anxiety. His courtroom experience had taught him to focus on the positive. "It sounds as if it is a raid for a number of people, not just individuals. Hopefully it is nothing more than a check for falsified identity cards. Hers is good. They can check with her family. They may just let her go, especially if she comes up with a believable story about the disguise. Marlise is smart, Barthold." His mind shifted to Ada and the baby. "Were they checking all the trains?"

Barthold looked up, uncomprehending. "All the trains? Yes, no one could leave the station."

"How did you get out?"

"They made way for me. Saluted me, for God's sake. We have to get Marlise away from them."

Alex tried to sound encouraging. "Maybe she was not blacklisted yet. If she is truly arrested, she will wind up in Scheveningen. I will visit the jail tomorrow and try to find out what happened."

Barthold's eyes lit up.

"But," Alex continued, "this will make it absolutely necessary that you move to your new place today. You move one by one."

"What about Marlise?"

"I will get a new courier for you. You will have to get rid of that SS uniform somehow. If you didn't look like such a natural in it, I would have thrown you out, for my safety and everyone in this building."

"The hell you would. You wouldn't openly throw an SS officer out into the street. I am asking, what are we doing for Marlise?"

First things first. Alex had to warn Ada and make sure that she and the baby board the train at another station.

But the younger man grabbed him by the arm. "Do you even hear what I am saying?" he hissed, shaking with anger. "I am talking about the woman I consider my wife. Right now I am disgusted with all of us, myself included, believe me. Do you know what Philip told the guys right in front of me? That we should shoot Marlise between the eyes if she is let go because they will follow her every move."

Alex gently lifted Barthold's hand from his arm. "Barthold, these are extreme measures. We will do all that we can for Marlise, I promise you."

Barthold stared him in the eyes as if looking for truth. "Do you ever wonder if we are wrong in what we are doing? Marlise herself hates guns. Don't get me wrong, she has strong principles. When the students went on strike, she was one of the first to speak in their favor. She worked on the underground newspaper and helps people in hiding survive because it is morally straightforward."

Alex folded his arms across his chest. "Many people are fighting Germany, and many are dying for it in the world." He had his eye on the clock, but he felt it was better to let Barthold open up.

"But we are not openly fighting," Barthold argued. "Yes, we are in a real war, but we have no uniforms, no rations, and none of the privileges of the Geneva convention. We're at the mercy of the Germans and the blunders the other side makes. Between the two they'll kill us all off. Think of *das Englandspiel*! How many of our agents will it take before London realizes the Germans have cracked the code? I can't help thinking that we don't matter."

Alex remained silent, listening.

"What I am saying," Barthold went on, turning toward the window, "is this: Is it worth it? Is it worth risking our lives and the lives of Dutch people who have nothing to do with all of this? Are we actually making a difference in this war? They said 85 percent of us students refused to sign what the Germans required. We were trying to protect Jewish professors and students. That's very different from what we are doing now. Because of me, Marlise is part of it." He slammed his fist on Alex's desk. "I have a friend who simply stays home and finishes his studies with the help of some sympathetic professors. I now believe that he is a lot smarter than I am. I could have done the same, working on a future for Marlise and me. It's my stupidity, and she is paying for it."

Alex thought of his own family. What would he choose? "Of course I have doubts at times," he said. He was surprised to hear the words he barely acknowledged to himself out in the open. "Sometimes I think we go on because we have no choice anymore."

Enough of this, he decided. He got up to hold the door open for

Barthold. Then he addressed him loudly in German: "Right now, we have to deal with an emergency situation."

That evening, he took the radio into his bedroom. The raid had been carried out by six British aircraft, a perfect example of successful precision bombing. Gestapo records were said to be destroyed, an action that would save countless lives.

At the registry office, 12 Dutch employees had been killed.

6

On his way to the jail, Alex tried to control his nerves. It wasn't only the risk in trying to locate Marlise, but also not knowing what Barthold and his friends might do. Or perhaps they had already tried to free her?

He was jolted out of these thoughts when he met Gunther and a group of austere officers at the entrance to the jail. Gunther immediately took Alex aside to vent his frustration about the precision bombing the day before.

Alex listened to his vituperation against the British and the resistance.

"How callous to kill their so-called allies! Twelve Dutch citizens dead!"

Alex was careful with his responses, keeping them as neutral as possible. The truth was that he was taken aback by the ruthless efficiency of the attack, yet he acknowledged that a warning could have been dangerous to the operation and would have cost more lives.

Suddenly, Gunther motioned him to enter the corridor. "I have sad personal news for you," he said in a low tone. "It appears that we are holding your niece."

Alex stood still. "My niece?" The image of his nieces, the oldest eight years old, flashed in his mind. Surely not the Jewish baby? Or Ada?

"The one who plays chess with you. As a friend, I feel sorrow for you. We believe she may have connections with the resistance."

Gunther led Alex through the corridor and down the steps to the isolation cells. At one of the doors he stopped. He shoved aside the shutter and peeked through the hatch. He beckoned to Alex to have a look. Sitting on the cot and staring straight ahead to the opposite wall was Marlise. No wig—her red hair was piled up on her head.

Alex spoke loudly, first in Dutch, then in German. "I don't know her, but she is a beauty."

Did her shoulders move slightly? He was conscious of Gunther's eyes watching him.

"*Ach ja, schade, solch ein schönes Mädchen.*" [What a pity, such a beautiful girl.] Gunther unlocked the door and walked in.

Alex held his breath. Would Marlise be up to the challenge? She turned and looked at them. Was there a darkening of the eyes, a telltale widening of the pupils, when she saw his face? But he need not worry. She turned her gaze back to the wall, offering them her haughty profile.

Alex's heart lurched in his chest. "Why is she here?" He was not prepared for Gunther's cold answer.

"*Da ist etwas los, das weißt man schon.* [Something is not what it seems, that much is clear.] But we will find out. They will make her talk." His tone changed. "Unless she is willing to cooperate..." He stopped and looked at Marlise, who gave a little cry.

She suddenly said in a hoarse voice, "I feel strange. I think I am going to faint." She slumped and slid down from the cot onto the floor.

Alex hesitated; he had learned to distrust every first reaction. But Gunther, surprisingly, had already bent down and lifted the limp body, placing her again on the cot. "Probably a lack of food."

Alex stepped back toward the door, where Marlise would not see him when she came to.

Gunther was still staring down at her. His face was inscrutable, but Alex heard him mutter, "I will make them bring her some milk and eggs."

Alex backed out of the cell and walked away.

The image of the German bending over Marlise's small body stayed with him throughout the day. When he unlocked his front door that evening, he felt watched. Who was spying on him? Who was willing to betray him, and her?

This time it was Alex who sat behind the unfinished game, anxiously waiting for Gunther to return. He ran through a mental list of all the people Marlise had come to know during her work.

Marlise had worked for the resistance in one capacity or another since the universities closed in 1941 after the student protest. With Barthold, she had joined a group working on one of the underground newspapers. Then, when Barthold joined a cell of the armed groups, she had remained with him, working as a courier. The question was whether it was now time for Alex to go underground. He was fervently hoping it would not be necessary. He could not imagine himself living that way.

He heard someone enter the front door, but this time Gunther went straight on to his room. This could be nothing but a bad sign! Alex stood up, wringing his hands together. Would now be his only chance to escape? To go through that door and leave everything behind? Would the Gestapo be able to decipher the information hidden in his files?

Something held him back. "I can't. Not yet," he whispered to himself. "I'll find out where things stand." Halfway up the stairs, he called, "*Herr Kommandant!*"

To his relief, Gunther opened the bedroom door and ambled down the stairs. "*Eine Minute, bitte.*" He walked into the study with a bottle under his left arm and two glasses in his hand. "The finest cognac, *mein lieber Herr Advokat.* I took the liberty of grabbing these glasses from your dining room. Please be my guest."

Was there a glint in Gunther's eye? He seemed to be in a surprisingly good mood. Alex sniffed the rich fragrance, deftly swirling the amber fluid in his glass, but he was afraid to drink.

They began to play. Alex took his time, wondering how to broach the subject that preoccupied him. He did not want to seem too interested in Marlise. What, if anything, did the man know?

But it was Gunther who brought up Marlise's arrest. "As to the political prisoner, I personally have taken on her interrogation. This will give her a chance to cooperate before the usual methods take effect. She will be well nourished during this time, I assure you. I could see that you felt pity for her weakened condition, and believe me, so did I. Her identity card checks out. She is from a prominent family in Wassenaar. Well educated, too. She told me that she was studying to be a lawyer like you, at Leiden University, and speaks German fluently." At this point, he waxed lyrical. "A perfect Germanic example of true Aryan stock. *Ein Edelweiß!* Why would such a splendid young woman become mixed up with subversive activities?"

"What makes you believe she is?" Alex said coolly, trying to sound noncommittal.

The German had color in his cheeks, his shoulders squared confidently, but his eyes were frosted glass. "I did not say she was. We think she may be. She is not cooperative so far. I have a feeling you don't agree with our beliefs, unfortunately. The Dutch people are very foolish. You are our Germanic brothers and could have been part of the Reich. The master race will prevail in the end!"

Alex took a sip of his drink. A warmth spread through his body. "She is not my niece," he said in a neutral tone.

The German did not rise to the bait. "She says she is not your niece. An error, *Herr Advokat*. I will take your knight. You should pay attention to the game. You are playing poorly tonight."

"It must be the cognac. I haven't had anything this strong in a long time." Alex took another sip. A dangerous anger rose in him. "You know, *Herr Kommandant*, perhaps the Dutch people do not see themselves treated as brothers. Why should they?"

Gunther looked down at the chessboard. He poured himself another drink and held the glass up to the light. "There were, and still are, choices. Some people joined us and were rewarded. We offered all your countrymen peace if you cooperated with us. But people here were deluded by Capitalist-Jewish propaganda. The Führer was right.

As our Germanic brothers, you became traitors to the Germanic race when you resisted."

"Traitors? To which country?"

Gunther sighed. "Not a country. The Reich does not recognize your little country. You are traitors to the Aryan race, our race. The Führer's plan of deportation should have been carried out back in 1941 to punish the Dutch people and to germanize Poland. An inferior race, the Slavs."

Alex remembered the bizarre project, which consisted of moving millions of his countrymen to the Polish province of Lublin. "It was true, then? We thought it was just a mistake of the propagandists to try to scare us."

Gunther moved a pawn. His eyes were expressionless discs, but his hand was trembling. "The Führer does not make mistakes. The people around him make mistakes sometimes. They put the plan on hold. And then the eastern front required our attention and efforts."

Alex took the pawn with his knight. "The people here are suffering," he said in a conciliatory tone.

"You are not suffering alone. The German people are suffering too. The terrible bombardment of our cities is inhuman."

Alex sat up. His head was on fire. He seemed to hear himself from a distance, as if someone else was speaking. "Did the Germans not start this type of warfare? Killing civilians, bombing cities? Maybe the Dutch haven't forgotten the flattening of the inner city of Rotterdam after the surrender in May 1940. That could make them suspicious of the Reich, *nein*? But then, it's all part of your new kind of war, Blitzkrieg, *nicht wahr*?"

This time it was Gunther's turn to flush in anger. He stared at the chessboard, then took one of Alex's black rooks.

Alex swiftly moved to block the king's escape and called it mate.

Gunther, conceding, stood up to leave, but before closing the door he said between clenched teeth, "That is *not* what Blitzkrieg was meant to be. You should be very careful, *Herr Advokat*, when you insult a German soldier."

Alex felt the blood drain from his face. The stark fear sobered him up.

That night, he pried loose the floorboards of the closet in his bedroom. He crawled in to try the space. He barely fit. Before going to bed, Alex hid the radio under the boards in the closet.

7

"You owe me, Henk. I saved your life."

Henk van Waarden finished writing a prescription. He put his pen down and stuck his glasses in the breast pocket of his white coat. "I may owe you my life, but not that of my children. My daughters are too young."

"What about the girl I saw here? Does she work with you?"

"Riena? She helps me out, and I teach her—an arrangement beneficial to both of us. She's a bright girl, Alex. She'll be a good doctor."

"What do you know about her?"

"I've known her since she was a baby. Actually, I delivered her. I trust her with my patients' secrets."

"The family? Are they 'right'?"

"They are our neighbors across the street, and probably safe. They're patients of mine and good friends. But not as old friends as we are, Alex." Henk stood up and clapped Alex on the shoulder. "Go ahead, ask her. If she wants to do it, I won't hold her back. If you need me as a contact person, I'm willing to do that for you, since you have the German in your house. But remember, she works for me first and foremost."

Alex leaned back in his chair. The walls of the small office were lined with glass cabinets. This was Marian van Waarden's domain, her dispensary. He knew the couple from their university days. They had planned it all then. Marian had chosen to open a pharmacy so they would be able to work together in their own home, raising a family in a quiet commuter village. Everybody envied Henk and wondered what Marian saw in him. She was beautiful, tall, and blonde. He seemed boring, reserved, and studious. But she knew all along what she wanted. No doubt Barthold and Marlise had believed in a similar future.

Marlise! What he had seen that morning perplexed him.

The guards had strict orders not to allow anyone near her. After several days of trying to gain access to her, he finally had succeeded.

Marlise was in the same cell, sitting on the cot. What stunned him was the sight of flowers. On the floor, between the door and the cot, a huge bouquet of red roses stood in a jar. The guard, obviously afraid, had pulled Alex away before Marlise had seen him.

The door to Henk's office opened and brought Alex back to the present. A slender girl walked in.

Sitting in front of him, in the light of a large window, Riena seemed too young to be a medical student. Her face, with its high cheekbones, had retained its childish outline in cheeks and jaw, with wide-set, dark eyebrows on a smooth forehead. It gave her an air of vulnerability.

"I can't imagine you were in university three years ago."

She laughed. "This would have been my first year. I am only a sort of errand girl here."

He lowered his voice. "That is what I am going to ask you: To do errands for me."

She scrutinized his face with clear green eyes. "Does it matter how old I am? I will be 20 in June." She had understood. He saw it in her changed expression.

"What you will be asked to do is dangerous, but there are other reasons why I would not ask someone who is too young. For example, right now I need a young woman to bring English cigarettes to a soldier in the SS Totenkopf Regiment."

"What are they for?"

Leaning back in his chair, Alex looked through the window. Marian van Waarden was stepping through beds of flowering daffodils and crocuses, picking a bunch of white narcissus. Her blonde hair reflected the sunlight.

"The cigarettes?" he began slowly. "Well, we have some contacts in that regiment—an Austrian, actually, who gets information for us in exchange for cigarettes. He bribes others there."

She thought about this, then asked with a searching gaze, "And how do the cigarettes get to this Austrian SS-er?"

"They are transported in a small suitcase or briefcase. You would act the part of the Austrian's girlfriend."

Her green eyes, contrasting with the dark eyebrows and lashes, were blazing now. "No. Never." She stood up with a toss of her brown mane. "For one thing, my father would kill me if he found out."

"But if he knew why..."

"Then he would most certainly kill me! He thinks he has enough to worry about with my brother underground."

Alex smiled. "You are exactly what we need. We need people who will not tell anyone, least of all their own family. Come and see me in my office tomorrow morning. You work afternoons, don't you?"

He made ready to leave. As he put on his coat, he said as an afterthought, "We will find someone else to act as the Austrian's girlfriend. You won't have to do that. And another thing: No one in the Underground has a last name."

Riena seemed flustered. "I am sorry. I suppose if you really need me..."

He interrupted her quickly. "How will you hide your activities from your parents, if you live with them?"

"That would be no problem," she said, with a tinge of bitterness in her voice. "My parents and I, we don't talk that much anymore. They never ask. My hours here are irregular. We just live and keep quiet." She seemed to want to say more but fell silent.

Henk stuck his head in the door to tell Riena that she could leave. The last patient had gone.

As she took off her short white coat, Alex was struck by the contrast between her graceful bearing and her ill-fitting, patched clothing. Four years is a long time to keep a growing teenager throughout in clothes that fit, he thought.

He held out his hand. "So, are you coming tomorrow?"

She nodded.

He left for the train station, feeling guilty.

Almost four years earlier, when the noise of air battles awakened Nettie and Alex before dawn that morning in May, his daughter had been a nine-year-old child. When he last saw her, she was taller than her mother. Four years! How long could this go on? Would there be a western front?

He took the train back to the city. As he disembarked, he felt uneasy. Train stations and trains were traps, after all. One's best chance of escape would be to run across the rails, but what a target! When he let himself into Ada's apartment, a neighbor opened her front door. She looked him over before she shut the door again. He felt exposed.

"They've got to move out soon," he muttered under his breath. He looked around Ada's living room. "Where's Barthold?"

"On receiver duty. If you want him..." Hugo said as he stood up.

"No, leave him. I'll get him later."

The others trooped in, having heard Alex come in. He left the news about Marlise for last. "Even with my guard connections in the jail, it is impossible to get to her. They are more afraid of the *Kommandant* than of anything I have on them."

"Why? What's going on?" Hugo asked.

Alex decided to tell them everything: Gunther's decision to conduct her interrogation himself and the bouquet of flowers in her cell.

Anton scratched his head. "What do you think it means?"

The others were silent, waiting for Alex's answer. "It can mean different things. We all know what red roses stand for. Maybe he simply fell for her; the man has a sentimental streak."

"Maybe they are a sign of gratitude," said Philip, "and that again could be for different reasons."

Leo's voice was low. "The best scenario for us is that he is a romantic and that she hasn't told him anything."

"What are the chances that he will let her go?" Anton asked, preferring not to continue their line of speculation.

Alex began to answer, but Philip interrupted. "If she is let go, we shouldn't let her get beyond the front step. They'll follow her, and we will all be finished, dead. We can't let it happen."

"She doesn't know this address or any other. Everybody has moved." Hugo turned to Alex. "Isn't that so?"

Philip glanced sideways at Alex, and said, "She knows Alex and where he lives."

Steven ignored the last remark. "With such tight security we probably won't know if or when she gets out." He turned to Philip. "But if I do, I sure as hell won't tell you."

Suddenly they were all arguing over each other.

Alex shouted, "Quiet! We have neighbors here. And Barthold—"

At that moment Barthold came in. "We have a message about a drop not far from here. It's for tomorrow night."

In abrupt silence, they moved to the dining room in unison and sat down around the table still covered with Ada's Persian rug. Elbows resting on the table, they began to plan.

Alex caught the eye of the young Englishman in a shared moment of relief. He was not needed any longer. Silently, Alex slipped out through the front door.

8

Steven was the unchallenged leader of the operation, but Anton drove the truck. They trusted him, the country boy, to drive without lights. Eyes burning with effort, Anton clutched the wheel. It was a winding, tree-lined road on top of a narrow dike built alongside a meandering river.

They had scouted the area in daylight on bicycles, but now the world had changed into shades of gray and black. The fields down below, barely visible between black tree trunks, were covered with a silvery blanket of low-lying fog.

To everyone's relief, Anton found the path down the side of the dike. The truck lurched into the fields.

"Good job, Anton." Steven was sitting beside him. "The ground fog looks pretty low. They'll be able to see the lights."

The field where they waited was wet with dew. The branches of the bushes around the open terrain were dripping.

They sat in silence, shivering more from tension than cold. Was that a sound in the bushes across the field? Were Germans lying in ambush? There was a rustling under the trees, followed by a raucous cry. Fearing detection, they held their breath. "An owl," Anton whispered. Was it startled by other humans? They listened, but there was only silence.

The next worst thing would be that the plane would not arrive. A part of the risk they took was perhaps to wait for hours in vain.

When the time stretched well past midnight, gradually the bushes could more readily be distinguished along the side of the open space where the drop was to be made.

They had "borrowed" a farmer's truck for the night, which they hoped to return before the farmer noticed it was missing. Transportation of the containers in a drop was a major problem because of their weight. It was fortunate that they had some gasoline, siphoned off a German truck by Philip. One had to admit that the guy had guts.

There was almost no wind. Sound would carry far. Was there a faint sound of an aircraft? Suddenly, they heard a plane's engine; right overhead, it seemed. They all jumped to turn on the lights of the truck and their flashlights. The rush of adrenaline erased all thought of anything but the recovery of the precious cargo.

In the darkness, they saw the outlines of parachutes descend and heard dull thuds on the soft ground. Then the plane lifted higher, and its sound became fainter.

"Nice job." Hugo spoke up in his enthusiasm, but Steven grabbed him by the arm.

"Quiet!" he whispered. "We wait here by the truck till we're sure there are no Germans here. We don't know if we're alone."

After what seemed like an endless wait, they ran as one toward the containers. They quickly folded the parachutes to be taken back and hidden. The containers were heavy, and the ground was soft and wet. It took all the strength they could muster to load the containers on the truck. Their clothes were soaked with sweat.

Anton, behind the wheel, kept close to the rough trail. "Hang on," he shouted when the truck shook dangerously on the incline to the top of the dike.

Steven tried to help him find his way along a back road to the village church, where the containers would find their temporary hiding place. But it was instinct sharpened by fear that led Anton in the right direction. To be found with the containers in the truck would be an instant death sentence. Besides weapons, the containers would hold medicine, a supply of cigarettes, and sometimes even bicycle tires.

At the church, they were let in a small side door by the minister, who seemed to have been listening for their arrival. Without a word, he helped them carry the containers. All manpower was needed to get them through the narrow door and down the steps into the cellar.

The church had the damp, intense cold of unheated old brick buildings. Even so, sweat dripped down their necks into their shirts. It was crucial to move fast; daybreak could not be far off.

Afterward, the minister locked the basement and let them out through the side door, which he locked with a large key on an iron ring. He pointed out the direction they should take back to the farm to avoid the main roads.

Once again in the truck, they could see contours more clearly. A hint of lighter gray in the sky was a reminder that daybreak comes early in spring. Anton started the motor and headed out toward the road, which was nothing more than a sandy trail in the grass. It was rough and difficult to see through the fog, yet it was easier now to stay on course in the faint light of early dawn.

When the dark hulk of the barn came in sight, the sky had changed to twilight, and tree branches were silhouetted against a dusky-orange sunrise. Anton parked the truck behind the barn, and they ran toward the road. Suddenly they noticed Philip was missing.

"He wants to siphon off the rest of the gasoline," Hugo whispered.

Steven ran back and, grabbing Philip by the shoulder, dragged him along. It seemed they all had escaped detection, but on the way to the road they saw a woman in front of the door. It was too dark to see her clearly, and she did not move or make a sound. She clutched a dark wrap around her shoulders. Her face was shadowed by a black shawl. They did not stop. They ran to their bicycles, which they had hidden hours before, or was it days? It seemed an eternity ago.

The only thought left for all of them was to get away.

9

She had an eerie feeling she had seen the man before. He was seated behind a desk with his back to the window, his face in the shadows. A mustache, thick glasses. Perhaps it was his voice that seemed familiar. She sensed that he was uncomfortable too. She took the documents and put them in her shoulder bag.

In the hallway, she looked at the bicycle. It was a man's bicycle, but she easily swung one long leg across to mount it. Riding this bicycle was like flying over the roads. What an exhilarating feeling to ride on good tires! Once taken for granted, the pleasure of it took on an entirely new dimension.

She sang a German love song, cycling under the new green and blossoms of the trees overhead. She tried to lower her tone—an effort to imitate the husky sound of Swedish actress Zarah Leander, whose sultry performances had impressed her and her teenage friends when they were exposed to German culture in the first year of occupation. From that time until all radios were confiscated, however, German programs had been all that remained available to them to hear.

It was a cool day, but bicycling warmed her with a feeling of happiness and confidence. At her first stop, she carefully padlocked the bicycle beside the house and then knocked on the window as instructed. In the semidarkness of a back room, she found an entire Jewish family gathered together. Faces turned to her, eyes luminous. The suspicion in the room was palpable.

She took the identity cards and ink pad from her brown leather shoulder bag. She could feel the reluctance in their hands when she took an index finger to make a print on each card. Nobody spoke, not even the children. Outside again, she breathed deeply. The sky had darkened. Windblown rain stung her face as she pedaled as fast as she could. She pulled the bicycle up the steps to Ada's apartment and wheeled it inside. The men undid and emptied the canvas bags strapped to her bicycle.

A dark-haired, broad-shouldered man she had not seen before was watching from a distance. She walked over, smiling, with an outstretched hand. "Did we meet? I am Riena."

His face seemed to break into a smile. "Philip. Come here, I want to show you something. Can you sew?" He showed her into one of the bedrooms. Heaps of fabric lay on the floor. "Parachutes. Real silk. You can have as much as you want. Make yourself a dress."

She knelt down and pulled the silk up to her face. It felt smooth and light. There was so much, and the richness of it! "It's beautiful," she murmured, looking up at him.

He had a grim set to his mouth, but his dark eyes looked friendly, watching her. "I'll find scissors, and you can take what you want." His tone was gruff, but the tenderness in his face was still there.

She wanted to explain that she was afraid to bring it home, but he had read her thoughts. "You can sew it here. I am sure old Ada has a sewing machine stashed away somewhere in a closet. Wait here."

"You'll look smashing in that frock this summer." The English words startled her. She had not noticed him sitting on the floor in a corner, his back against the wall and legs stretched out in front of him. Still on her knees, she slid over to sit beside him. "I am Riena."

"I know. You are the angel of mercy. My real name is Hugh. I hate it when they call me Johnnie." He had a boyish grin. Making an attempt to stand up, he flinched in pain. "It's the bloody ankle. I must have sprained it. Changing position still bothers me."

"Let me see. Sit down and take off your sock, Hu… yueh?"

Her attempts to pronounce his name made him laugh. "You'd better stick with Johnnie. Ow! Take it easy, will you?"

The ankle was still multicolored, but Riena saw that it had little swelling. "It's not broken, as far as I can tell," she reassured him. "Rest and put your foot up. It's the only cure."

"Well, I get plenty of that in this first-class sanatorium."

She laughed, placing her hand on the injured leg. "It's going to be all right."

Suddenly she noticed Philip standing in the doorway with a pair of scissors in his hand. He was frowning.

"I was checking his sprained ankle," she said quickly. "I work in a doctor's office. Didn't you know?" Why did she think it necessary to make excuses to Philip? Why did he look angry?

He threw down the scissors and pulled her up. Together they walked back into the room, his hand lightly on her shoulder. She was aware of the surprised stares of the others.

They were sorting through the contents of her bicycle bags on Ada's dining table. The food would be strictly rationed.

Doctor van Waarden had given Riena a message for Barthold from the parents of Marlise: Barthold was not to contact them. Above all, he was not to try to contact Marlise "until all this is over." The message included no explanation. Upon hearing it, Barthold kicked a chair so violently that it fell over.

Riena did not know Marlise, and Barthold's passionate reaction surprised her.

The young man named Hugo tried to reason with him. "Maybe it means she is safe. It won't be long now until the invasion. They are sending us weapons to be ready for it. We'll all be free."

Steven seemed to echo the feelings of the entire group: "It would be best if we split up and moved away from here. How much did they get from her?"

"Leo and I are getting ready to leave anyway," Anton said. "We're waiting for a new moon and quiet weather. We have to plan how to get from here to the boat."

Riena sat down at the table and watched the faces of the men around it. The imminent invasion: where would it be? The

Netherlands and Belgium were a possibility, but the Westwall built along that stretch of coastline was thought to be the most impenetrable.

"I don't think it will be here," Hugo said. "The Germans are threatening to put the provinces of North Holland, South Holland, and part of Friesland underwater if the Allies invade this area."

"They're just bluffing. Scare tactics." Steven brushed this specter aside.

"I don't think so," said Hugo. "They have put much of Zeeland underwater already." His fiancée lived on one of the islands in that province, so this was personal.

But Steven stopped his friend. "The problem right now is how to get Anton, Leo, and Johnnie through the German defense zone to the North Sea. The sooner we deal with it, the better. Leo is at the receiver, but Anton can fill him in later. We should inform Johnnie of the pros and cons of the trip."

"Smart idea. We can't afford to let him back out, only to walk over to the nearest German barracks to report as prisoner of war and explain where he's been for the last few weeks, now can we?" Barthold drawled. "I'll get him."

Riena noticed now that Hugh's walk was somewhat stiff, but his face did not betray any pain. He sat down beside her.

Steven addressed Hugh in English: "Are you prepared to risk a crossing to England in a small rowboat with two of our people? It is not all that far. The downside? To start with, just getting to the boat will be risky. The dunes are full of land mines, and they have built concrete blockhouses and bunkers all along the beach. It is crawling with German military."

The Englishman nodded.

Steven arched his eyebrows. "I didn't tell you the worst of it yet. Most of the guys who tried never made it. Some probably drowned, and others were likely shot. If the Germans pick you up, they won't ask questions. You'll face a firing squad if they think you are one of us. On the other hand, you can continue to stay with us and wait out the war." With a crooked smile, he made a grand gesture of welcome.

The Englishman grinned back. "No, thanks! Anything but that. I'm in."

They hesitated, looking at Riena who stood up to leave. "I have some work to do in the other room."

She was cutting a large swatch of silk when Hugh came back. He pushed some of the fabric aside and sat down on the bed. "I want to ask you a favor." He reached inside his shirt and handed her a piece of paper, folded many times. "My Mum and Dad. Their address."

She sat down beside him. "What on earth can I do?"

"When all this is over, you can reach out to them. I may not make it. They'll want to know. They're both past 60, and I am their only son."

"Of course I will." It was strange that she could not imagine a world in which she'd be able to do such a simple thing. She took his hand. "I wish... I hope you'll be all right."

"A handshake? What about a goodbye kiss?"

He put his arms around her and kissed her hard on the mouth. She could feel the stubbles on his chin.

"What's going on in here?" Philip stood in the doorway and stared at them.

"We're saying goodbye." With both his hands in hers, she gave Hugh a light kiss on the cheek and joined Philip, who walked her to the front door.

"When will you come back to make your dress? The others here - their girlfriends like that silk stuff, so don't wait too long." Philip stepped back and opened the door for her.

"Don't worry," she answered, wheeling the bicycle out. "I'll be back soon."

The waiting room was full of patients. Doctor van Waarden was brusque, although the people were patient and quiet, even the children. Hungry children don't waste much energy, the doctor had explained to Riena.

She knew that it bothered him that he could do so little to help because of the lack of medicine and supplies, such as bandages. Skin infections were rampant from a lack of soap, hot water, and the most rudimentary disinfectants.

When Riena had finished, Mrs. van Waarden called her in to join them for a meal in the dining room. She served boiled potatoes with small tender spinach leaves fresh from her garden.

Riena sat down gratefully. She felt as if she had never tasted anything better in her life.

10

"There is this German supply truck with just one driver," Anton said. "He delivers potatoes and such for their kitchens. Lottie says it's a regular route. I say we take it to get through to the beach."

"What do we do with him?" Steven asked.

"Nothing at all. He goes inside, and when he comes back out, the truck will be gone."

"In broad daylight?"

"Not really, he comes around early in the morning."

"Where do we leave the truck? And who will drive it?" Steven liked precision, but he could see the potential of the plan. However risky, it was better than the paralyzing tedium of waiting.

A new recklessness had taken hold with the arrival of spring and a stretch of mild, sunny weather. Being cooped up in the apartment was torture. They had taken turns getting out of the apartment for walks, although the risk of being picked up by the Germans was ever present.

Steven knew that Anton had met his new girlfriend, Lottie, on one of these excursions. Sometimes Anton had stayed overnight at Lottie's apartment, where she operated a hairdresser salon. She did not know, and did not want to know, where Anton lived.

The most dangerous part was getting in and out of Ada's

apartment. Neighbors might be wondering what was going on. Most would simply choose to ignore, but not necessarily all; some people still sided with the Germans, or perhaps were simply afraid of having a resistance group as neighbors. Beyond that, there were supposed financial rewards for alerting the Gestapo—meaningless promises, because the stores were empty.

"I'll drive the truck and wear the SS uniform," Barthold volunteered. "My German is good. I'll let the three of you out near the beach, where you can hide in the bushes for the day. I know a road north of here where it is quite wooded going through the dunes. And then I'll drive the truck back and abandon it."

Steven weighed the risks. "We should all go, just in case we have to shoot our way out of there."

It turned out to be surprisingly easy. It was as Lottie had said. The driver was alone and left the truck idling, key in the ignition, while he went inside.

That was the signal for them to emerge from their hiding place in a narrow alley. It was crucial to move fast. Luckily nobody seemed to be watching. When they jumped into the truck, the guards were at some distance from the road.

Barthold drove because he was familiar with the road. Steven sat with the others inside the shaking and rattling canvas-covered truck. Across from him was the young Englishman, his boyish face beaming with excitement. He wore a pair of Hugo's pants and one of Anton's sweaters over his own shirt. Only Philip was missing; he had stayed behind to man the receiver.

"She was right—bags of potatoes! Maybe we should take some, huh?" Hugo laughed. "Wait! Here are some boxes. Medical supplies, it says. Should we open one and see what's in there?"

"Let's dump it all at the Red Cross hospital afterward," suggested Steven. "I've heard they're out of food." He peeked out from under the canvas. The truck was now moving through a deserted, built-up area. Citizens had been evacuated to make room for German fortifications. "Nobody is stopping us. I guess the fog will help us."

The truck turned onto a road leading through the wooded dunes. Steven remained on the lookout. They passed a warning sign with a skull and crossbones, the emblem of the SS regiment occupying that area. Then the truck lurched to the left.

A chain had been hung across the road with another warning sign, but Barthold passed that, too, with the left wheels in the sand of the dunes.

Then, suddenly, an abrupt stop.

Steven heard Barthold swear, "*Verdomme!*" That was definitely not German. The door opened, and Barthold ran to the rear, his face pale in the gray fog. "Look at this. A tank trap!"

They all jumped out. The truck had stopped a few inches from a gaping precipice. The excavation was about 20-yards wide and ran the width of the two-lane road.

"No way to go around, either." Steven looked at the high barricades of triple-rolled, spiked wire on both sides of the road. "I'm sure that goes on forever, with land mines all along it."

On the other side of the trap, they could vaguely discern the continuing road. Left and right, the wall of barbed wire stretched into the distance. The sides of the tank trap were steep, reaching groundwater down below.

"This is as far as the truck goes," Steven said matter-of-factly. "What do you guys plan to do?"

"How far is it to the beach?" Anton asked.

"At least five miles," estimated Barthold.

"Well, I'm ready. We have the whole day." Leo examined the sides of the man-made ravine. "The three of us will have to help each other down and up."

Anton rummaged through the truck and came out with a piece of rope.

"What's happening?" asked Hugh. The freckled face of the young British pilot was drained of color, his eyes dark with anxiety.

Steven responded brusquely: "Are you going or staying? They're going, so make up your mind, and good luck. We'll wait till you're on the other side before we head back."

Going down was the easy part. Leo, Hugh, and Anton were already sloshing through the water. After an interminable wait,

Steven, Barthold, and Hugo heard a faint okay from the other side of the tank trap. In silence, the remaining three went back to the truck.

Barthold drove again, faster this time. The fog was lifting. The truck stopped in front of the hospital. Hugo and Barthold jumped out, and Steven stayed in the back to hand down the supplies. Working quickly, they dumped the potato sacks and boxes of medical supplies near the gate. A couple of nurses passing by stared at them in surprise.

Steven tapped on the driver's door. "This is the Sportlaan, not that far from Ada's apartment. Should we leave the truck here?"

Barthold started the motor. "Jump in. I'll turn into a side street and let you out before I return it."

Later, standing in the side street, Steven and Hugo hesitated before taking off. Steven looked up at Barthold, who still sat behind the wheel of the truck. "You're bringing it *back*?"

"Well, as close as possible. I want them to believe it was all for the potatoes."

Steven grinned at the sight of Barthold in the gray uniform looking down at them, his eyes shadowed by the captain's cap he wore. He made a perfect German officer; he was a bit too stylish for a potato-truck driver.

"*Richtig, mein Kapitän!*" Steven made a mock salute before heading home. "Let's go."

As Steven and Hugo returned to Ada's apartment, Barthold parked the truck a couple of blocks from where they had first seen it. Leaving the key in the ignition, Barthold stepped down into the sunlit street. Nobody paid attention to him.

But later, a neighbor shook her head in shocked surprise when she thought she saw a German officer letting himself into Ada's apartment.

11

"Now we have two uniforms to get rid of, a German and a British."
Barthold stood leaning against the doorpost, looking at Riena.

She was seated behind Ada's sewing machine, intent on her work.
It was an old black treadle machine, so the whirring sound stopped
when she lifted her toes to pay attention to him. "What do you think
we should do with them? I'm new at all this."

"Don't take this lightly, my girl. Both are equally incriminating."

Drawing on a hand-rolled cigarette, he watched her. He had
recently taken to smoking the Ersatz tobacco he had repeatedly
cursed in the past. Riena got up and opened the window to dispel the
pungent smell. The whirring sound resumed.

Barthold added: "The best thing for you is not to have anything to
do with all of this. Much as we enjoy your presence, you should not
waste your time on us."

Suddenly Philip came into the room. He looked from Riena to
Barthold with a frown. "I finished my shift. It's all yours."

But in the same bantering way, Barthold continued, "And what
you see in this man is beyond me. He is dangerous, I tell you. We
don't know anything about him. We suspect he killed the SS officer
who wore that uniform. A violent man, Riena. Listen to my words:
don't trust him."

Riena gave them a wide smile. "But that is what intrigues me in a man, the depths of secrecy and danger." She got up and closed the window again; it was rattling in the wind. "My, it's a cold wind, and this is June."

"They won't try anything in this weather," Philip said in a somber tone, looking at the dark clouds chasing across the sky. "First we hear that the invasion is close, and then they wait until the weather makes it impossible."

It was true that there had been a spell of fine weather in May, but the first week in June had brought belated spring storms.

Philip sat down on the bed. "It's your turn at the receiver," he said curtly to Barthold. "Steven and Hugo have gone out. They took the night shifts."

"Why do you hate him so?" asked Riena when Barthold had left.

"I don't hate him. I despise him, and maybe I envy him. I can't talk to a girl like he can, so smooth with his suave manners. He makes you laugh."

"But I like you because you are different and serious, Philip. There is this aura of mystery about you. Is it true that you are a communist?" She pulled the silk up to her mouth and bit off a thread.

Philip appeared to hesitate. "I am a Marxist. Have you ever read Marx? You should."

Riena stopped the machine and turned to him. His dark eyes had an imploring look—pleading with her, a girl barely out of school. She felt flattered; he was a man compared to the others, lanky youths still. He had a big head, massive shoulders, and a deep bass voice. It was strangely touching.

"Perhaps I will," she said. "All we ever learned in school was his name and how he and Lenin started the revolution in Russia." She tried to imagine Philip as a schoolboy, poring over political tracts. "How old were you then, when you became interested in all that?"

"I started reading Marx in school, as a teenager. It was boys like Barthold who made me feel like I did not fit in. I did not dress or talk right. My father was a dockworker in Rotterdam." He looked at her with defiance. "He was a foreman and earned more than some of those boys' parents, those uppity lawyers."

"Oh, that's where your accent comes from, Rotterdam." Riena walked to the mirror, holding the dress in front of her. "It's much too long," she murmured. "As far as clothes go, Philip, war is a great equalizer. That's why I learned to sew, for better or worse."

"Is it finished?"

"No, I have to try it on and hem the bottom. Could you help see if it hangs straight?"

She slipped out of her skirt and pulled her sweater over her head. Standing barefoot in her white cotton slip, she shivered in the cold. The silk dress billowed over her head. She pulled it down and looked critically in the mirror. It had a simple square neck and showed off her small waist.

"I can't do buttons or collars," she said. "That's why it has such a low neck." She climbed on a chair and handed Philip a piece of chalk from Ada's sewing kit.

"Will you please mark off the length? Really short is fashionable now in Paris, I hear. Just above the knee. Don't be silly, Philip, my knees are here, not halfway down my calf. Thanks, I really appreciate it."

She jumped down, smiling at him, but her face froze because of the look on his. "Philip?"

His voice seemed to come from deep inside him. "Will you just let me hold you close for a moment?"

She willingly moved into his arms and put hers around him.

"God, it's been so long," he murmured.

When she looked at his face, his eyes were shut tight. Then he suddenly let her go, and she was left feeling cold and forlorn. She hastened to put her warm sweater and skirt back on.

He went over to the window, turning his back to her. "You're one of them. You belong in a different world."

She put her hand on his arm. "Why? Where do you belong?"

He looked angry, pulling his arm away. "You live in a dreamworld, a girl in a fairyland. It's time you wake up to what's real, for God's sake."

"Don't talk to me as if I'm a child. You know where I live? In a foggy world of uncertainty about the future. I don't even want to consider the future because I might start to believe there is none. But you did not answer me: where do you belong?"

"As a child, I did not belong with people like you, and when I finished university in Amsterdam I did not belong at home either." He gently touched her cheek. "You better go. The storm is getting nasty."

Riena slept fitfully that night. In semiwakefulness, she saw Philip mouthing words, but she couldn't hear them. Were they warnings or threats? The storm didn't help. The windowpanes rattled as rain whipped them in gusts.

Coming down the stairs in the morning, she heard excited voices in the front room. She threw the door open. Neighbors were crowding the room.

Her mother ran to her, tears running down her face. "Riena! The invasion! It has started! They've landed in Normandy!"

In an instant, Riena felt catapulted into a new universe.

12

Alex looked at the clock and tuned in to London.

In the exciting days since the invasion in Normandy, he had seen little of the *Kommandant* and had been able to resume his habit of listening to Radio Oranje in the evening. Each time, he carefully returned the radio to its hiding spot under the floorboards in the closet.

The front door slammed. With his hand on the radio, Alex listened. Then he heard the familiar sound of boots in the hallway.

"*Herr Advokat*, are you there?"

Alex pushed the radio under the blankets, closing his eyes in frustration. "I am resting, *Herr Kommandant*."

Gunther knocked on the door and entered without waiting. "So early! I was hoping to find you up. I thought you might want revenge."

Stunned, Alex turned to face him. "Revenge?"

"I mean a *Revanche Partie* of chess." He looked at Alex sitting fully dressed on the bed. "At least you haven't turned in for the night."

Alex stood up. "All right, why not?" He was conscious of the radio still hidden under the covers when he followed Gunther down to the study.

Gunther carefully placed the white pieces on the board. "What news of the front have you heard?" he asked suddenly.

Alex waited for a split second. "People in the streets say the Allied forces are making progress," he replied, trying to sound casual.

"We know Normandy was a diversionary tactic." Gunther moved a pawn. "The real front will be farther north. We are ready for them."

Alex stared at him. The German seemed smug and calm. It was an effort to keep from trying to shake his confidence. But the Germans were still around, with their guns and power. Indeed, even in Alex's own house Gunther still had total power over him.

Alex's stomach churned. He turned his attention to the game, but Gunther insisted: "The Dutch people are smiling and happy, but as a friend I want to warn you: Don't be confident. The Führer is holding the winning cards."

Alex tried to control his urge to reply, but sheer curiosity edged him on. "Some of my countrymen believe that it will be difficult for the German armies to have sufficient forces on both the eastern and western fronts, especially because the Reich has to keep occupying armies in so much of Europe. They believe there will be peace talks soon to prevent further bloodshed."

Gunther pooh-poohed this with a wave of his hand. "We are entering a new phase of the war, my friend. We have new weapons so powerful that we can force the conditions of peace."

"You mean Hitler's secret weapon we heard so much about?" Alex tried to keep the irony out of his voice, but it did not escape Gunther.

"Exactly, my dear friend. Secret weapons, fortunately for you and your countrymen. Because if we go down, so will you."

Alex laughed. "You mean we lose either way. Are you saying that your unmanned rocket is the secret weapon, the *Vergeltungswaffe*, to save the Reich?" He saw Gunther's expression change, so he quickly added, "I just wonder why you are so sure the English will buckle under your revenge weapon, since they didn't do so during the London air attacks three years ago. Things looked much worse for them then."

There was no reply. They continued to play in silence. Gunther remained grim faced. Finally, after midnight, Alex called it a draw, but the German made no motion to leave.

Leaning back in his chair, Gunther said, *"Mein lieber Herr Advokat,* perhaps it is time for us to talk more openly."

Alex felt his heart thumping.

Gunther continued. "I can be helpful to you if you can be helpful to me. You see, I am a friend you have right here, in The Hague. *This* is the place where you may need help. London, Berlin, and Washington are far away. You and I do not even consider Moscow." He gestured to the four corners of the small room, and bent over toward Alex, his eyes hidden behind his glasses. "What do the Allies know of our reality? Nothing."

Gunther waited for an answer, but when Alex simply shrugged and nodded noncommittally, he went on. "You and your countrymen are worth less than the pawns on this chessboard to the men in power—Churchill, Roosevelt, Stalin, and our Führer. You remember *das Englandspiel*?"

Alex closed his eyes. The subject was too painful.

"My countrymen, Major Hermann Giskes and *Obersturmbannführer* [senior assault-unit leader] Josef Schreieder, did not have much trouble with British intelligence, did they? The British played right into their hands. How easy it was for the British to sacrifice all those Dutch agents. How many again? A hundred?"

"Almost half were French or British," corrected Alex. But was a reply possible? The England Game had lasted two years despite all the warnings transmitted to London. It seemed to be an unbelievable blunder, or was there a more sinister explanation? Its devastating effects had reached as far as the French resistance.

Gunther was clever. He seemed to know just where the sore spots were.

Alex let the silence hang between them until Gunther spoke again. "What about the invasion in May 1940? Did the British help you to defend your country? All they did was sink your ships in the harbor. Did you see any of them then?"

Alex tried to hide his irritation. The man was overdoing it.

"I am a simple soldier, *Herr Advokat*. We have a lot in common.

We both live in dangerous times and want to survive to be reunited with our families. I am offering you my friendship in return for yours."

Alex stood up and said, "I will remember your offer."

"I hope that neither one of us will need it," Gunther replied.

The German rose politely to leave, but Alex noticed a distinct air of satisfaction, almost a smile, on his normally expressionless face.

13

It was almost dark in the small café, although the sun was still in the sky. Alex was waiting in one of the wooden cubicles reserved for discreet encounters. In normal times, one could meet a mistress there for a drink or perhaps meet a client who wanted privacy. Every now and then, he pulled out his watch from his waistcoat pocket. The man was late. How long would it be safe to wait? But suddenly he was there, sliding into the seat across from Alex, his eye on the tiny blue-and-gold leaded window.

He leaned across the table so Alex could hear his whisper: "The directives from London are to unite and cooperate."

Alex arched his eyebrows. "Really? And how, may I ask? It is easier for them to direct than it is for us to accomplish." He thought of the various loose organizations across the country that differed in ideologies and political leanings.

The man tossed his comment aside. "We are to plan a meeting of key people to get ready for the liberation and for what will happen after the war."

Alex made a gesture of impatience. "Good God, that is the stupidest thing I've ever heard—bring everyone together to be murdered in one fell swoop. Why don't they tell us how to get through this war?"

"Keep your voice down. We're talking about an order from the government-in-exile. Apparently the Allies are intensifying the weapon drops and training of the underground combat groups."

In an instant, Alex felt electrified. "It's true then. We're close." Dizzying images of freedom and normal life flooded his mind.

The man lowered his voice again to a whisper. "There is something else. The German resistance has sought contact with us. They are planning another attempt to assassinate Hitler, followed by a coup in Germany to prevent further bloodshed and destruction. Some big names are involved."

"What would that mean for us?"

"Of course we would demand that the whole German civilian administration and military be moved back to Germany. All surviving Dutch prisoners in concentration camps should be sent home, including the involuntary workers in Germany. Unfortunately, we'll probably never get back everything that was looted from our country."

"What about the Dutch Jews they deported?"

The man shifted in his seat. After a silence, he gave a hesitant answer. "Alex, they don't want to talk about them. It seems as if they are no longer there."

Alex looked into the man's eyes but had trouble accepting what he saw in them. He felt a chill run through him.

They did not speak again.

Holding his hat down, Alex hurried home in the twilight.

Light was seeping in under the door of his study. He had not seen the *Kommandant* for a few days, but here he was, looking at the books lining the walls.

"I was concerned about you, *Herr Advokat*. It is well past curfew time. You are taking chances."

The locked filing cabinet was untouched.

Alex made an effort to speak in a friendly manner. "The spring is making me careless. Nightfall is late now."

The chessboard had been moved. Through the glass tabletop, the hollow in the foot was visible.

Gunther followed his gaze. "A perfect hiding place."

Alex went over to the bookshelves. He took out a few books and from behind them a flat wooden cigar box.

"This is an easier hiding place. I can't offer you cognac, *Herr Kommandant*, but I can offer you a genuine Havana from before the war."

Alex unhooked the lid and held the box out to Gunther. A faint smell rose from the cigars. They were flaky with age.

Gunther removed the gold paper band from his cigar and clipped the end. He slowly drew on it till the tip glowed. "A memory from better times, *Herr Advokat*. I appreciate your sharing it with me."

Alex placed the chessboard in the center of the table again and sat down.

They played in silence, thin wisps of blue smoke circling around and drifting to the ceiling. Alex played carelessly, but he noticed that Gunther too was distracted; he took an extraordinarily long time to consider each move.

In one of these pauses, Gunther laid his cigar on the rim of the ashtray and looked up at Alex. "Do not make an attempt to visit the redheaded girl in jail again, *mein Herr Advokat*. She is no longer there."

Alex lowered his eyes to the game. A hundred questions raced through his mind, but he was afraid to ask any. In a moment of carelessness, Alex sacrificed both bishops, and in a few more moves he lost. He heaved a sigh of relief when Gunther left. How much did the German know? What had happened to Marlise?

He went downstairs and stepped outside onto the back terrace. The smell of honeysuckle hung in the air. Its sweetness was almost too much to bear.

"I'll try to phone Nettie," he said to himself. "That'll calm me down."

14

"They've all gone," Philip said, "to a new place. I waited here for you."

Riena tossed her hair back from her damp face. It was a warm July afternoon. She was wearing a sleeveless blouse and shorts—too short, her mother had said with a frown, and who'd want to spend priceless coupons on shorts? She looked around the strangely tidy apartment. "I haven't finished the dress yet. I meant to wear it home today."

"You're not worried about your parents?"

"I'll tell them it belongs to a friend. We borrow from each other all the time."

She walked into the bedroom where the treadle machine stood with the unfinished garment draped over it. The French doors leading to the narrow balcony stood ajar. Late afternoon sun flooded the room through the net curtains.

"Hemming the skirt by hand will take time," she said. "But as my mother says, it looks so much neater than doing it with the machine. So, what is the new address?"

Philip sat down on the side of the bed, watching her sew. He took a long time to answer. She looked up from her work. He was staring at the floor, his elbows on his knees. "I don't want to tell you," Philip said. "This is your chance to get out. Take it, and forget about us."

She dropped the dress. "What exactly are you telling me? Don't they trust me? Do you not want me around?"

Next thing she knew, he was hugging her hard, kissing her forehead, eyes, and mouth. His intensity surprised her. Although she was almost as tall as he, he picked her up and carried her to the bed. She grabbed his wrist in a reflex when he put a hand on her leg.

Philip stretched out beside her and leaned on his elbow. "Don't worry, whatever you want. Do you have a boyfriend?"

"Yes... no. I have always had boyfriends." Being so close to him in the bright sunlight gave her a curious sense of displacement.

"Oh, I forgot. Girls like you don't do such things. You just tease the poor guys. It didn't take you long to turn that English boy's head."

Indignant, Riena sat up. He rolled onto his back, his hands behind his head. "A couple of months in medical school would have taken care of that daddy's girl's innocence. Is your old man going to pay the bills?"

Riena lay down again, looking at the patterns of light on the ceiling. "He says if the communists overrun Europe, they will always need doctors and engineers. My brother studied engineering at Delft until the student strike."

It was true that it seemed as though the Allied invasion was stalled while the Soviet offensive made fast progress.

Philip turned to her and began stroking her hair and shoulder. "A practical man, your father."

She laughed. "You wouldn't like to hear what he truly thinks of that future. Are you really a member of the Communist Party?"

Philip's dark eyes looked away across her shoulder. "I signed up when I was at the University of Amsterdam. We both did."

Her heart seemed to stop. What was he saying?

"I was married, Riena. My wife is dead. I am a 30-year-old widower." He turned away to get up, but on impulse she took his hand with both of hers and pressed it against her chest, where her heart was beating. Philip put his face against her skin in the hollow between her neck and shoulder. She heard a dry sob and thought she felt the dampness of tears. She had never felt closer to anyone.

Sometime later, he began to caress her waist and pulled up her blouse. She wore no undergarment. Her breasts were small but firm in his hands. "Don't be afraid. I won't hurt you."

His touch was knowing and tender.

They were naked now, kissing in the golden light. She felt vulnerable and yet drunk with an unknown power.

She heard him murmur near her ear, "So smooth—a different world. I'll be very gentle." His knee pushed her legs apart. She felt the roughness of his legs against her inner thighs. She began to stroke the back of his head, his neck, and his back. She felt as if she had joined humankind.

When she was dressing, it was late. How could so many hours have gone by?

Philip, on his knees in front of her, put on her shoes. "I want you to make a decision, Riena. You can stop here and now."

She went into the hallway, where she had left the bicycle. "No. Give me the new address."

Philip examined the bicycle. "A man's bicycle! What kind of *Ausweis* do you have for it?"

Riena reached in her shoulder bag and handed him the official-looking document, stating in German that she worked as a telephone operator for the Wehrmacht.

Philip compared the document's identification number to the number on the bicycle. His face reddened. "This is a different number! German soldiers are requisitioning bicycles everywhere now, especially ones like this, with good tires. You are not safe with this piece of useless paper. Promise me to ask for a new *Ausweis*. God, this makes me angry." He was trembling. "If I tell you the new address, swear to me that you will work with me. You need to learn how to defend yourself from the Germans and dilettantes like this." He held up the piece of paper and slapped it with the back of his hand before giving it back to her.

She smiled at him, but in truth she was in a hurry to leave. Her parents might question her. She promised and blew him a kiss. She left the bicycle in the shed of the van Waardens' and walked across the street.

Her mother's look made her painfully conscious of the dress. She tried to run upstairs, but her mother held her back. "Riena, that dress hasn't been properly hemmed. Don't go out like that again."

15

"It is finished, little fellow."

The little boy, blond and blue-eyed like his mother, banged with both hands on the table of his wooden high chair. It made the spoon and bowl jump.

His mother wiped his face and lifted him out of the chair. She was a tall, gaunt woman; thinness did not become her. Muffled sounds of gunshots could be heard through the floor.

"They are practicing with the new guns," the woman said. "If you want to go down to the cellar, Riena, you'll find them there."

Riena sat down. "Something is going on in the city, Greta. A lot of soldiers are around. It looked like they were putting up loudspeakers on the street corners." She shivered. "I wonder if it has something to do with the attempt on Hitler's life yesterday."

The little boy ran around, pulling a toy on a string. Suddenly he stopped to listen. Strains of music came through the open doors and windows.

"The *Horst Wessel Lied*," said Greta. "It's the Nazi fighting anthem."

They heard an announcer, and then, unmistakably, the fanatic voice of Adolf Hitler. The long-drawn, high-pitched sounds were unleashed in fury.

The boy started to cry. Greta picked him up in one arm and began to close doors and windows. "There is not a soul in the street," she said. "You better stay here till this is over."

They exchanged glances over the boy's head.

"Greta, do you ever wonder what this is doing to us? Will we ever be normal people who speak freely and do things spontaneously? Most of all, will we ever really feel again? It's as if there is a glass wall between me and the world; I can see what's going on, but I can't feel it."

"We will never be the same. We'll never feel things as we used to. But you, Riena, you were just a child when this started."

"I know. Since the occupation I've grown up with the resentment of anything German. I wonder if we'll ever get rid of this hatred." Riena stood up, fists clenched. "All I have is anger. Over and over, I dream of killing this man. Is that normal? I stand in front of him, emptying a revolver into his body. I don't even know how to shoot."

Greta rocked the little boy in her lap. "Killing Hitler? There would be others. It wouldn't solve anything." The insistent whine of the intolerably stretched sounds still reached them through the closed windows. "I shudder when I think of what they'll do to these men and their families. But you want to become a doctor. You should be thinking of saving lives, not killing."

"I think I'll be a good doctor, a good surgeon even. The glass wall will keep me from being swayed by emotions."

"What if the patient is a German soldier? Or an SS officer?"

"I would be totally dispassionate. That is, until he's cured." Riena laughed and stood up. She went down to the cellar, which stretched underneath the entirety of the old house. A man with a British accent showed the men how to use the new guns. The back wall was marked for target practice.

Philip put his hand on her shoulder. "I'll show you how to use a revolver. I think you can handle this one."

Riena was aware of the disapproving glances from the others. The instructor did not seem to notice and included her without question. She was a fast learner, with a sharp eye and a hand steadied by grim determination.

Later, Barthold was the only one to comment. "The cold steel of guns does not become the lady. By the way, you have no right to look so devastating in your parachute dress." He winked at her.

She knew that the pale color of the natural silk contrasted with the deep golden glow of her skin and hair, brought out by the summer sunshine. She was getting prepared for the ride back when Philip joined her in the backyard, its high wooden fences covered with climbing yellow roses.

He gave her a lingering kiss. "You look really pretty in that dress," he said. The hunger in his eyes made up for the clumsy compliment. His big hands easily encircled her waist.

"We have to go to a new address, an apartment downtown," he said. "We can't stay here much longer. There are rifles, hand grenades, and quite a few handguns here. It's too dangerous for this family. Someday I'd like to find my own place so we can see each other more often."

He helped her get on the bicycle. She adjusted the wide skirt to swing her leg across. He patted her knee and said, "Nice tan on those long legs. Good thing there aren't any young men in the streets."

She blew him a kiss and, tossing her hair back, rode off.

The loudspeakers had disappeared, but ahead she heard the rhythmic thudding of soldiers' boots. Turning a corner, she came upon a troop of German soldiers marching in full gear. She heard the familiar command screamed at them: "*Eins, zwei, drei, vier, ein Lied!*" [One, two, three, four, a song!]

As one man they sang, with a sound that was sullen yet disciplined. "*Auf der Heide blüht ein kleines Blümelein, und es heißt Erika!*" [On the heath blooms a little flower, and it's called Erika!]

Riena passed them, submerged in the raucous cadence of their singing. A physical unease gripped her, perhaps produced by the seemingly endless thunder of boots hitting the pavement and the deep vibration of the many male voices. She was acutely conscious of the dress, as if draped in a flag or the silken cape of a matador. Hurrying along, she felt their eyes on her long after she had left them behind.

16

From a distance Alex saw her approach, walking between the dripping trees. She had her hands in the pockets of her raincoat, her shoulders hunched. He went toward her and put an arm around her. "Thanks for meeting me here, Ada."

"Oh Alex!" Her face was drawn.

They walked over the cobblestones, slippery in the rain.

He pulled her arm through his to steady her. "Tell me how it happened."

"They knew about her because they had picked up her father and little brother. Everybody in that house was arrested—all the people who were hiding them and the other illegals, Jewish or not. The next morning the Gestapo were at our door. I suppose they must have checked out the mother's relatives." She took out a handkerchief to wipe her eyes. "I told them they'd have to kill me first, but they just shoved me aside and took her away."

Alex looked at the government buildings reflected in the gray water of the pond. "Was anyone arrested at your place?"

"No. In our case it was different. Some of them were those wretched collaborators, militia types from the village, who knew the family. Maybe that shamed them. I told them I was the only one to blame, but they didn't want me. They took her—a baby! It breaks my heart. All I can do is pray. Who am I to question God's will?" She blew her nose. "I can't help but wonder, how powerful is the devil? Why does God allow it?" She stood still to face him. Her complexion, normally so rosy, had become sallow. "Where will they take her and her brother?"

"Ada, don't torture yourself. You've done what you could." He felt uncomfortable, remembering her warning.

"But I do blame myself. Why didn't I bring her back to The Hague when I could?" She began to walk again, as if unable to stay still.

"Because with the western front so near, we thought you'd both be better off in the country. Who could have thought they'd still be rounding up human beings?" He was at a loss for words.

"You didn't answer my question: where are they taking these families?"

Alex walked faster to catch up with her. "First they go to one of the local transit camps in Vught or Westerbork, most likely Westerbork. From there…" He took off his hat and wiped the wet rim with his sleeve. "Who knows, the western front may save them from being deported to Germany. With the Allied armies closing in, they may still be in our country when the war is over."

"What have you heard?"

He looked around. There was no one near, but he lowered his voice anyway. "They're close to Paris. Everything there is on strike, and the Americans have landed on the French riviera. France will be free soon, Ada."

"How about us?"

He sighed, looking up at the sky. "From what I gather, the Canadians and British are heading in this direction, northeast along the coast. It's just about over for us, too." He hoped it was true.

The rain was letting up. A dull sun was reflected in the water, now rippling in a light wind.

"Let's walk around the pond," Alex said, "and then toward my office and a tram stop for you." He took off his raincoat and hat. The fresh breeze felt good. "It must be nice to be back home, Ada." He was looking for something comforting to say, but she began to cry again.

"It's so empty. Oh God, I can't stop thinking about her."

He put both hands firmly on her shoulders and faced her.

"Don't. Try not to think about it. It will kill you." He handed her his handkerchief.

Gradually her sobs subsided. She wiped her eyes. "Oh, I'm so sorry. I forget how lonely you must be. You are very patient."

"You must have hope. My sources told me that sometimes partly Jewish children get better treatment than fully Jewish children. Maybe that will keep her and her brother safe."

"Like in the beginning, when the Germans advised the Jewish council in Amsterdam to cooperate." Anger dried her tears. "Hope! It's an abomination, all of it."

Her outburst surprised him; it was so unlike her. "A couple of months more at most, and it will all be over. Keep thinking of that."

She fell into step beside him. The August light already had the wistfulness of late summer.

Strolling along the Noordeinde, they passed the front gates of the royal palace. Although the building was left empty, German sentries stood on guard in front of it. Inside the gates, a man in uniform barked orders at a group of subordinates.

"There still seem to be a lot of troops around," Ada said. "The end may not be that easy."

He helped her into a streetcar and walked along the Zeestraat to his office. Her words kept ringing in his mind. The future was a no-man's-land of uncertainty. It was better not to think. If only one could turn off the merciless procession of thoughts.

17

"I'll stay with the receiver," Hugo said. "Have your breakfast tête-à-tête."

Steven was grateful. Thea had come from Amsterdam to visit him on the two days she had off work. Her schedule in the hospital was demanding. They rarely saw each other now; it was a luxury to have time together.

He had fallen in love with her when he was 16. Although a grade below her in school, he had been a lanky youth towering above her. She was dark-haired, small, refined. Even now, she barely reached past his elbow, but he never ceased to be amazed by her inner toughness. He felt content and stabilized as he watched her precise movements and listened to her cheerful chatter. The trip from Amsterdam had been far from comfortable because passenger trains had disappeared. She had stood the whole way in a covered freight car, where the smell was nauseating.

While talking, she put golden-green apples in a bowl on the kitchen table, where they caught a ray of sunlight. The summer had brought more variety to their food supply, although it required exhaustive trips into the countryside.

"It's nice that the farmers are willing to let you have all this produce," she said, looking at a shelf with potatoes, carrots, and onions.

"Usually, they're not. It helps that we have guns."

She sat down. "What are you saying?"

"How else do you think we're surviving here?"

He knew that startled expression of hers. This was not an argument he'd wanted to initiate. She was going to make this difficult.

"Look," he continued, "we've settled this among ourselves. Hugo and I have decided we'll only raid farmers who are collaborators or politically on the wrong side of the fence. This is a war after all, and we are fighters."

"How about Philip?"

"Philip? He just goes his own way. It's all the same to him. The haves have to share with the have-nots, like it or not."

No doubt that was why Philip had left in the small hours, to forage for food. It was better not to question his methods.

"And Barthold?"

"He will have no part in it. He still eats the stuff though, albeit under protest."

Barthold in particular was violently opposed to taking food from farmers. He called it "nothing but highway robbery."

Steven recalled the bitter arguments when he and Hugo had attempted to find a middle ground by agreeing to raid only certain farmers. To Philip, these were the finer points that were easily overlooked; it just added to his contempt toward Steven and Hugo. And Barthold would not budge from his standpoint either.

Steven did feel grateful to Barthold for giving up his bed to Thea. Barthold had volunteered to spend the night in Lottie's beauty salon nearby, which had become a second refuge. Lottie had kept in touch with them, hoping to hear news of Anton. Of course, the desire to give Steven and Thea privacy was secondary for Barthold, who wanted to avoid the pain of being around a couple.

"How dangerous is it to go out at night for food?" Thea wouldn't let Steven off the hook yet.

Steven thought of the frightened faces in the light of a torch or flashlight. The image made him feel uncomfortable. He showed her a hole in the wide sleeve of his windbreaker. "A bullet hole. The last guy had a rifle."

She turned pale. A silence fell between them.

"Let's go for a walk. It looks so nice out," Steven said as he put the dishes in the sink.

"Do you think...?" Thea was hesitant.

But Hugo called from the back of the apartment. "Go get some fresh air, you lovebirds. I'll hold the fort."

The morning was cool, with a light west wind from the sea, but it was warm enough in the sunshine to stroll leisurely along the canal under trees heavy with aging foliage. Crossing a bridge, Thea spotted a secondhand bookstore. "Steven, please, I have to look for a book. I promise I won't take long."

Steven was resigned to following her inside. He looked through old prints of sailing ships and became interested enough not to mind the time spent. Every now and then he looked up and saw her dark head bent over the shelves, still searching.

Suddenly she was at his shoulder with a wrapped book under her arm. "Shall we head back?"

Arm in arm, they turned a corner to walk toward the side street where the apartment was.

Then he saw it. A crowd was gathering at the entrance to their street. He took Thea by the hand and started running toward it. Through the mass of people, he saw green helmets.

There were soldiers; he couldn't see how many. They had blocked off the street entrance at both ends. Two armored Gestapo cars were parked in the middle of the street, guarded by soldiers pointing their rifles at the crowd.

All thoughts left his mind. He felt his heart beat in his throat.

Suddenly he saw six armed soldiers with Hugo between them. They came out the door, onto the sidewalk. Hugo looked up and down the street. His face was small and white. The soldiers pushed him into one of the armored cars.

At that moment, Steven became aware of where he was. He turned around and glimpsed Barthold in the crowd. They exchanged a glance and fled in opposite directions. Steven still had Thea by the hand, but at the first side street he pushed her away from him. "Go!" It was the first word spoken between them since they had left the bookstore.

He kept running without looking back. He refused to think beyond the present danger.

All day and night he ran and hid, seeking cover in the city wherever he could, like a wild animal captured in a cage.

18

Steven heard the bell ring. He checked through the window and opened the door.

Greta pushed the large English pram into the hall. She lifted the child out and carried him into the front room. "All the weapons are still there," she said.

The boy held on to his mother's neck with one little arm, looking in turn at each of the strangers, Steven, Barthold, and Philip.

Greta had just gone to check on their apartment and had found everything untouched. Earlier, Hugo had been taken completely by surprise.

"It's a trap," her husband said. A quiet man who usually stayed in the background, neither had he offered, nor had any cell member asked, his name, nor any identifying information. "They are waiting for you to come back for the weapons. I'm sure they know how many of you were living there. Obviously, they were ready for all of you, with two armored cars." He frowned as he looked at his wife. "What were you thinking taking Robbie back there?"

"It's all part of my plan." There was a defiant, stubborn look on her face. "I promise you, though, I won't take him again." She put the child in a wooden playpen and knelt beside it to comfort him when he loudly complained. She stood up, turning to her husband. "Are you taking them over this evening?"

He nodded.

It was understood that Steven would go first.

He and Steven walked together through the darkening streets.

"Greta is up to something," he said. "I know that expression. Every bad thing that happens makes her more determined. Women think they can get away with anything."

Steven looked sideways at his companion's face. It was too dark to see his expression. "She seems to get away with a lot. Where are we going?"

"I am bringing you to stay at Noordeinde Palace until we find you a new apartment. Don't worry, you should be safe there with the Germans guarding it," he said with a dry laugh. "We'll go in at the back, through the gardens."

He unlocked a door in a stone wall, lining a narrow street. Steven followed him past the royal stables and over damp grass between hedgerows and trees.

Inside the palace, Steven was met by a white-haired man who took him up to the second floor. Without turning on lights, the man moved with the certainty of one who knows his way. He unlocked a door and gave Steven the key.

It was a bedroom furnished in opulent Victorian style, with a canopied bed and a window facing the front courtyard. Heavy velvet draperies obscured most of the glass, but standing to the side and a few steps back, Steven could just see the gate and the German guard. From the point of view of someone standing in front of the gates, Steven was in the right wing.

Adjoining was a smaller room, a boudoir decorated in a more feminine, frilly style, where the man pointed out a receiver. An old-fashioned marble washstand with running hot and cold water stood in a corner.

Steven sat down in the dark beside the receiver. It was small and could fit easily under the mattress if the need arose.

After several hours, he heard a knock on the door. It was Barthold.

"That took a long time," Steven said. "I was wondering if you'd make it."

"We were delayed." Barthold went over to the window. "There was a message from Alex. Hugo was executed last night. They don't even bother with the semblance of a trial anymore."

Steven fought to banish the intolerable images from his consciousness. He sought refuge in anger, saying, "What difference would a trial have made? He was a sitting duck—sitting on a pile of weapons when they walked in on him."

"Let me tell you about the weapons, Steven." There was awe in Barthold's voice. "Greta has been sneaking them out in the baby carriage. She piles them up under the baby's blankets. After you left, she went out twice."

Steven inhaled sharply between his teeth. "She is some woman. What does her husband say?"

"Not much. She is going back three more times tomorrow, she says. They're hiding the weapons in their cellar. We'll have to transport them to a different apartment."

"Is Philip coming here?"

"No. It's just the two of us. We thought it'd be better to split up from now on. Someone clearly saw us as a group and betrayed us."

"How did Philip escape that morning?"

"He was at the other end of the street. He got there at about the same time we did."

Suddenly Steven felt exhausted. He began to yawn. "Will you take a turn at the receiver first? In four hours I'll be ready to take over."

He stretched out on the canopied bed and fell into a deep sleep for the first time since the morning of Hugo's arrest.

19

From the radio came the sound of crowds cheering.

Alex walked back and forth in his bedroom, his fists clenched in excitement. This was reality, far more so than hearing the voice of an announcer from London.

This jubilation came from people like him, who had been through the same misery.

It was the third of September, a Sunday, and the voices came from Brussels, liberated that day. Belgium's capital was so close and yet so far removed from Alex's own reality at that moment. Would The Hague be next? Radio Oranje signed off with the message that liberation for them, too, was imminent.

With trembling fingers, Alex opened his bedroom door, but looking back he noticed the radio still exposed on the blankets. He rushed back and carefully hid it under the closet floor.

Monday was a day of suppressed excitement. The news traveled through the city by word of mouth. Strangers smiled at each other, pressed hands, whispered on street corners.

In the afternoon, his secretary knocked, came in, and shut the office door behind her. "Mr. van Vechtelen, do you have a moment?"

In all these years, they had never called each other by their first names, although he felt great fondness toward her.

"Of course, Miss Kuiper. Please sit down."

They smiled at each other. Leaning forward, she said, "If you have a radio, you should go home and listen. They are in Antwerp now."

"It's happening! If they move through our country as fast as they did through Belgium, we could be free in a week. How are your parents?" Although he knew she was living with her aging parents, he had never thought to ask her before.

"As well as one can expect, I suppose. But soon things will be easier. Have you heard from your family?"

"No, but it's a comfort to know that they are better off in the countryside." For weeks now, he had not been able to reach Nettie. He reached for his coat and hat. "I'll follow your advice if you do the same."

He followed her down the stairs and out onto the street. For the first time, he noticed how much she had aged. She had lost a lot of weight, and her hair was almost white.

The house was empty when he came in. It was deeply satisfying to think that soon it would be fully his again. He walked through all the rooms with a new appreciation. It was as if he had come back from a long journey and saw the place with fresh eyes. Nettie and he had shared a taste for the elegance of old furniture. Many hours they'd spent searching at auctions and in antique shops.

He ran his fingers along the smooth surface of the mahogany dining table. There was a thin layer of dust. "I have to get a housekeeper in soon," he said to himself.

In the evening, he went upstairs to his bedroom. He pushed his dresser against the door; only the bathroom doors had locks in their house. In his family, they had respected each other's privacy. Even the children had learned very early on to ask for permission before entering.

The exertion made him feel hot, so he went into the adjoining bathroom to wash his face. The bathroom had a second door leading to the hallway, which he locked. Feeling safe, he settled on the bed and tuned in to London.

It had been a day of euphoria, but he was not prepared for what he heard next.

The prime minister of the Dutch government-in-exile began his speech saying that the Allied armies, in their triumphant advance, had crossed the border into the Netherlands. Incredulous, he tuned in to the BBC and heard the strains of the Dutch national anthem. He switched back to the Dutch broadcast and thought he caught the name of the city Breda, in the southern province of North Brabant.

Close to midnight, he tuned in again to the BBC broadcast. There was no doubt. It was announced again: the city of Breda had been liberated.

In his excitement, Alex tried to phone Nettie, but he could not get through. The house remained still. The entire city was still, as if waiting. He pushed the dresser back against the wall.

After a few hours of sleep, he woke to the rumble of heavy vehicles in the street. He rushed to the front window in the hallway. In the gray light of dawn, he saw German troops passing by. It was a strange mixture of vehicles. Trucks, motorcycles, and armored cars pushed ahead, passing soldiers on bicycles. There were men's, women's, and even children's bicycles, with here and there a farmer's cart drawn by a horse, all manned by soldiers.

What did it mean? He looked at the closed door of Gunther's bedroom. For the first time in six months, he turned the knob and looked in. The bed was smartly made. If he had not spent the night there, where was he?

The phone rang.

Henk van Waarden's voice cracked with excitement. "The Germans are all going east, Alex, to the German border. The railroad stations are full of collaborators and their families trying to catch the last trains east. The resistance in Rotterdam has started taking back buildings."

"If Breda was yesterday, it should be Rotterdam today." Alex repressed a tinge of anxiety. Where were the liberators?

He was in the kitchen busying himself with breakfast when he heard the front door open. Gunther stood in the doorway, his face gray. "This is not the end for us," he said.

Alex laughed with contempt. His disappointment on seeing the *Kommandant* was so deep that he forgot to be careful.

Gunther's face colored a deep red. "I have been your friend. We made a pact to help each other. I hope you will remember that agreement if the Allied armies do get here."

Alex trembled with rage. "A pact? That's a lie! If you're still in my house when they get here, I'll hand you over so fast..." He stopped.

Gunther put his hand on his holster.

They stood facing each other.

Then Gunther turned and left.

The day passed in a whirlwind of rumors and breathless waiting.

It was evening when he heard the doorbell. In front of him stood Marlise. In shocked surprise, he pulled her inside. She was vibrantly alive, looking better than he had ever seen her. He picked her up like a child, twirling her around. "My God, I am happy to see you," he said.

They embraced, laughing and crying. There was so much he wanted to ask her, but the main thing was that she was there, living and breathing.

"Where's Barthold? Is he all right?" She waited, her hands folded as if in prayer.

"He is fine, but at the moment I don't know where he is. Give me until tomorrow to find him for you. Stay here as long as you want." He couldn't get enough of looking at her. Health had infused her with a beauty that took his breath away. The contours of her face had softened; her eyes and fiery red hair had a new sparkle.

She smiled, apparently enjoying his open admiration. "I am so lucky I made it here," she said. "South of the great rivers, the railroad strike has begun. We could hear the fighting."

Holding her hands between both of his, he listened. She'd been hiding on a farm in Zeeland, where her father was born and where her family had spent summers. There had been much concern about flooding, especially on the island of Walcheren. The Germans had shown signs of disorganization in the last few days.

"The *Kommandant* released you?"

"They were holding my father. I don't know what was agreed on between them, but I was released with him. My parents told me not to show my face again until the war is over."

"It is over now, and you are here. We have to celebrate."

They searched the house and found a package of pumpernickel and cheese. Alex remembered seeing the bottle of cognac in Gunther's room and went to get it. It was half full.

After they clinked the crystal glasses, Alex raised his glass to her. The cognac heightened the color in her cheeks. "You are a beautiful woman," he said. He couldn't take his eyes off her. "What's lacking is music." Trying to break the spell, he went to the record player. "We have some American records. Appropriate, don't you think?"

A few notes of an orchestra, and then the husky voice of Nat King Cole rose. They both laughed happily. "It's a surprise, the voice of an American on the other side of the world saying those words." Marlise couldn't stop giggling with delight. Alex swayed to the music.

"This hurts. It makes me think of dances before the war." She hummed to the music. "And I am once again with you."

"You're too young to feel sad about memories. There is a lot more for you yet." He pulled her up and began to dance slowly, holding her close. He had to bend down to press his cheek against hers. His knees weakened, but it was wonderful to know that his body had not forgotten to respond. He loosened his hold on her, and they sauntered to the table with the drinks.

Marlise took a sip from her glass. "There are Germans patrolling, Alex," she said, looking out the window.

It was getting dark. He couldn't see anything.

"Really, I saw them. They were holding rifles."

He turned off the record player. "Let's go upstairs, just in case. We'll listen to the latest news. Bring your glass."

On the stairs, he had to keep her from stumbling and felt far from steady himself. He turned on his reading light and threw open the doors to the balcony.

"Let there be light!" he shouted. "It's over! Are you listening, *Schweinehunde*? Go home! We are free!"

She giggled. "No, Alex." She staggered over and began to let down the heavy blackout curtains.

He helped her. "You're right. We want privacy."

They embraced again. She responded to his kisses, her cheeks aflame. He sat down on the bed and pulled her on his knee.

"I love Barthold," she said, almost dreamily.

"I love my wife. But oh, you're so desirable." He pulled her closer. "Nobody will know."

That was the wrong thing to say.

She wrenched free and stood near the door. "No," she said, "this isn't right. I don't want to."

He stood up and grabbed her arm. "You want it as much as I do. Don't act so prudish. The old *Kommandant* must have had fun, huh?"

Tears streamed down her face, but her eyes were dark with anger. "So that's what you think, what Barthold thinks? Let me out of here!"

"No, please listen. I don't know what came over me. For all we knew, you were dead." She was quiet now, still sobbing. "Marlise, please understand. I think highly of you. What happened today... you made me feel alive again. I'd forgotten."

Suddenly, he heard the front door slam. There was shouting in German, the sound of boots on the steps. He pushed Marlise into the closet, in the space under the floor. There was no time to replace the boards properly.

Alex was still standing with his back to the closet when Gunther burst into the room, flinging open the door. He looked around the room, at the bottle of cognac, the two glasses. Alex felt as if nailed to the floor. Gunther drew his revolver and stormed into the bathroom.

He came back and threw Alex aside. Standing in front of the closet, he began to shoot through the closed door. He aimed the last few rounds at an oblique angle, as if aiming for the closet floor.

Trembling, Alex stood against the wall. It's the end, he thought.

Gunther faced him, still holding the gun.

"A girl," Alex said. "She is gone. It's a long time since I've been with a woman."

Gunther put the gun back in its holster and said in a menacing tone, "For you and your countrymen, *mein Herr Advokat*, the war has just begun." He turned on his heel and stormed out of the room.

Sometime after he had left, Alex pulled up the planks. Marlise was hunched against the far end, holding her leg. There was blood on the floor. She was able to stand up. He carried her to the bathroom and wrapped her leg tightly in towels. Putting pillows under the wounded leg, he made her lie down.

His mind tried to grasp what had happened. Obviously, they were back, and the *Kommandant* was back in his house, now openly his enemy. He felt as if he would never sleep again.

They spent the rest of the night on the floor together, waiting and listening behind the locked doors of the bathroom.

20

Marian van Waarden crouched over the open fireplace, stacking twigs crosswise. Everybody stood close to capture some warmth from the only source of heat.

Alex, shivering in his damp clothes, looked out through the rain-streaked windows. The weather was relentlessly wet and stormy this fall. He wondered how much this accounted for the slow Allied progress south of the rivers. On certain days, they could hear the rumble of fighting from the front. Since the failed attempt to take the bridge at Arnhem, the front ran right across the country.

In the province of Zeeland, the fighting was fierce. The news had just reached them that the RAF had bombed the sea dikes that protected Walcheren, thus flooding most of the island, with the intent of eliminating the German defense line. The messenger was none other than Anton, now going by Tony.

"How about the civilians?" Henk van Waarden wanted to know.

"Most people survived by fleeing to higher ground," Tony explained. "They had been warned by pamphlets thrown from planes, but it was impossible to get off the island because the only causeway was constantly attacked. The Canadians are having a hard time; many have been wounded or killed."

"Arnhem is even worse off," said Marian. "So much blood and

destruction, and all for nothing."

"The Germans are looting the city now, punishing them," added Tony.

After the debacle in Arnhem, a gloom seemed to have fallen over the country, matching the dark autumn days. Food and fuel supplies were grinding to a halt. Fear had replaced the hope of the early days in September.

Alex looked at Anton. He had changed in the barely six months he'd spent in the free world. He had filled out and stood up straighter. His blond hair was cut in English military style, and he had returned with an English name. Five months of intensive training had prepared him for the role of agent. He exuded health and confidence.

It made Alex wonder what they themselves looked like to an observer from that other world. He looked around. What a pitiful lot they were now, himself included.

The railroad strike had started on the same day as the Allied offensive thrust in the middle of the country to get across the rivers. The joint British-American operation had started in Eindhoven, well south of Arnhem, and progress had been slower and much more difficult than foreseen. The bridge at Nijmegen was in Allied hands, but the Allied soldiers who reached the north shore in Arnhem either died or had to withdraw.

The timing of the railroad strike had not gone unnoticed by the occupying German administration of the Netherlands. In retaliation, food and coal transport to the west was halted, except to supply the Wehrmacht and to keep the polder pumping stations operational. After all, the Germans had no intention of putting the entire west of the country underwater while they were still there. Did the exiled government have any idea of the consequences when they called the strike?

It seemed to Alex that the agents, too, had been sent prematurely. Surely, organizing armed resistance made little sense unless the liberators were expected to arrive the next day, so to speak.

Alex, no longer able to contain his irritation, asked, "What can a few thousand lightly armed amateurs do against more than a hundred thousand trained German troops?"

"Sabotage." Tony was confident, almost cheerful. "Our government-in-exile has given us the go-ahead to commit acts of sabotage against the German army."

Alex noticed the sneer on Philip's face and felt it mirrored on his own.

"Like Putten a week ago." Henk's tone was heavy with sarcasm.

Tony was on the defensive. "Putten? I don't think that order came from London. It was a local decision to attack German dispatch riders. They were surprised by the shoot-out they found themselves in. After they killed one German officer, they let the others go—a strategic error."

"But the reprisals!" Marian cried out in obvious exasperation. "Killing seven people to set an example! Not to mention burning the village down and taking all the men and boys to a concentration camp in Germany—600 are missing. All for one damned German. It was Lidice all over again. Do you really think the Wehrmacht cares who gave the order?"

The image of the small village of Putten suffering this kind of revenge disturbed Alex anew. Who'd want to be responsible for such an outcome?

"The truth is, we are not responsible," Steven said, placing his hand on Tony's shoulder. "The Germans are, and they'll pay for it someday, I hope. We cannot give in to that kind of blackmail."

"There is one other thing," Philip said. "How do they expect us to do anything when we're on a diet of... tell me, Doctor, what is it now on our food coupons? Five hundred calories a day?"

"They're aware of it. Some supplies will be coming in from the south and east for resistance fighters, but it will be minimal, probably just enough for one meal a day. The logistics—" Tony interrupted himself. "Where is Barthold?"

He turned to Alex, but Alex looked at Henk, who said, "Barthold took Marlise to his parents' home in Overveen. Marlise had come back from hiding in Zeeland. I treated Marlise for a flesh wound before they left." Henk put more wood on the fire.

"What? Was she wounded in Zeeland?" Tony asked.

"No," Alex answered. "She came back about a month ago, when

we all thought the Germans had left. That crazy Tuesday, when the reports from London were wrong about the fall of Breda, we saw the German troops leave, but they turned around at the border." He saw the puzzlement on their faces. "Marlise came to see me. I thought the *Kommandant* had left for good, but he suddenly returned. I hid her under the floorboards of the closet, but Gunther started firing at everything like a maniac, especially at the closet floor."

"That's right." Henk nodded. "We found a bicycle for Barthold and they took off on it, Marlise on the rear rack. It's quite a ride, but we know they made it safely. That's where they will be for a while. We asked Barthold to get in touch with our underground telephone operation to report back."

"It's your turn now, Tony. Where is Leo?" Alex asked.

"He impressed the British in London and has become an important man. He was in the Arnhem area when the first paratroopers came down. He's good; I always knew he would be. Leo is very smart, you know." Tony's voice expressed admiration.

"We've got quite a cache of weapons and ammunition in our new apartment," Steven said. "If you want to start your operations from there, join me."

Looking out at every turn for German patrols, Alex rode home. His bicycle with its patched tires had become even more precious now that the trains and trams did not run anymore.

As on other evenings, he barricaded himself in his bedroom. He and Gunther had not spoken since that Tuesday in September, but his presence in the house loomed larger than ever. Gunther had set up an office in the living room, and a steady stream of soldiers' boots blackened the rugs in the hallway.

Alex tried to keep warm by wrapping himself in his blankets while he listened to the noises downstairs. Loud voices rose up from the dining room. A party? He flinched at every slammed door, every chair scraping on the parquet floor.

He heard a crash and then loud laughter. A German voice shouted obscenities. A wave of fury washed over him. He had to confront Gunther face to face.

He threw the blankets off and ran downstairs.

21

Riena pushed her bicycle along row houses, all alike. She looked at the numbers above the doors. She turned and walked back. Had she missed something?

A young boy, no older than ten, approached her. "Riena?"

She had never seen him before. She followed him into one of the homes, down a hallway.

He pushed open a door and said, "She's here."

There were two people in the semidark room, a woman and a man with a fake mustache and nose attached to dark-rimmed glasses. The woman was talking in a halting voice and seemed to be trembling with nervousness.

The man listened calmly and reached over the desk to hand a sheaf of papers to Riena.

"Here are the blueprints they've asked for." He smiled at her.

The difference in their demeanor was striking. Riena wondered if their disagreement involved her.

Still feeling a trace of unease, she set out through the city streets. As she entered an area away from downtown, her anxiety deepened. Lately, the streets had become quieter, and here not a soul was outside. Turning a corner, she saw the reason why.

On the street corners, soldiers were putting up machine guns.

97

Others with rifles on their shoulders were marching down the street, banging on doors and yelling, "*Aufmachen!*" [Open up!]

A raid. She rushed on. As far as she could see, it was only in this part of the city, most likely a search for young men to work in the German armament industry.

This is nothing really new, she tried to reassure herself. She had heard of more ruthless methods used in cities in the middle and east of the country.

In particular, she thought of Apeldoorn on October 2, threatened with bombardment if the men between 18 and 45 did not report to the German authorities. Eleven thousand did so after the bodies of ten resistance fighters were displayed in the city.

October was almost over, and so far the larger cities in the west had escaped the worst of such atrocities.

She was now approaching the concrete wall, generally known as the *Mauer-muur*, that the Wehrmacht had erected at all entrances to the city. To make the point clear, they had painted the word *Mauer* on it, the German word for wall. Under it, perhaps in an absurd effort to impress the wall's existence on the people's awareness even more, was the Dutch translation, *muur*. The name *Mauer-muur* had stuck.

Through the wall was a narrow passage. Riena was completely taken by surprise when a young German soldier stepped forward. "*Ausweis!*"

Time stood still. With sudden intense clarity, she saw a second soldier beside a few bicycles leaning against the wall on the other side. Down the road were two more soldiers, checking the papers of an elderly couple.

Her leather shoulder bag contained her identity card and *Ausweis* for the bicycle but also the blueprints. She forced herself to control the trembling of her hands.

"*Ausweis!*" he shouted again.

She handed over the *Ausweis* for the bicycle.

"*Personsbeweis!*"

She gave him her identity card.

He studied both, comparing the picture on the identity card with her face. In a dreadful moment, he bent over to compare the number on the bicycle with that on the *Ausweis*.

"*Da stimmt etwas nicht.*" [Something's not right.]

She had never seen anything in a sharper light. They were standing in the afternoon sunshine, in a brisk wind. He was freckled, young, probably her age.

Looking in his eyes, she wordlessly beseeched him: *Please, let me go.*

He looked around at his companion, who was checking out the bicycles against the wall. Then he looked at the two other soldiers, who were still occupied with the elderly couple.

"Where are you going?" he said. "I mean, there is another checkpoint at the railroad crossing. Can you avoid that?"

Life streamed back into her body. "Yes, I can. I will."

He handed her the papers. "Because you have such beautiful eyes."

Shakily, she mounted the bicycle. It was important to get away quickly, but not in an obvious hurry. Her legs seemed foreign to her body; she had to force them to obey. She could not betray him, or they would both be lost.

Well before the railroad crossing, she turned off the road. She rode along the tracks for a few kilometers and dismounted. Pushing the bicycle through the soft sand was harder than she had anticipated. She crossed the railroad bed, lifting the bicycle over the rails and stumbling over the rusty gravel. Her arms and legs wouldn't stop trembling.

Doctor van Waarden was waiting for her outside at the back of the house, his face tense. He gave her a searching look.

"Come and sit down; you need to rest. Have some water." Taking her shoulder bag, he checked the contents. His expression was grave. "Tell me exactly what happened at the *Mauer-muur*."

"You knew?" She was stunned, exasperated.

"We were warned through the underground telephone system, Riena. We have to know."

"But you couldn't warn me?"

"You had gone before they manned that checkpoint. Have another sip of water. Now, tell me, how did you get through?"

He listened attentively. When she had finished, he laughed and said, "I don't know why we even bother making you girls an *Ausweis*."

It was unsettling. Were they checking up on her? She was too tired to dwell on that thought.

She sat in her room, staring at the wide expanse of darkening sky. The sun had set, leaving an orange stripe between gray cloud banks that rolled in from the North Sea.

She knew she'd never forget that young soldier's face. He probably saved my life, risking his own, she mused. Under those anonymous helmets and uniforms, there are still some good people, capable of their own ideas. Who would have thought! He was Wehrmacht, though. If he'd been SS, he never would have helped her.

She shivered and pulled a blanket from the bed to bundle herself up. Philip was right; she'd have to get a new *Ausweis* with the correct number before making any more trips. A thought formed despite her efforts to suppress it: if she'd been caught, who'd be to blame?

22

It had been years since Alex had been in a car. At every turn, he shut his eyes. Traffic rules did not mean anything to this driver.

Alex was sitting in the back seat beside Gunther. In front were the driver and a soldier with a rifle.

When the car turned into a gate, he recognized the location. It was the country home of a Jewish colleague of his, gone underground with his entire family.

The guard at the gate let them through. Huge ancient beeches, their smooth bark a mossy green, flanked the house. They drove up over a thick layer of golden-brown leaves.

It was inside that the house had become unrecognizable. Alex had been there just before the family went into hiding. They had made the surprising gesture of having a farewell party for family friends. Alex had no idea what had happened to them since.

The entrance hall was bare of furnishings now. The walls had a dirty blackish look, and crudely drawn skull-and-crossbones markings were everywhere.

Gunther took him into the family's former music room. The son and daughter had played the piano and violin for their guests that night of the party. Alex was more moved now than he had been then, three years ago. He remembered the strange mood of the party. We suspected so little then, he thought.

Now the room echoed with emptiness, bare except for a desk and a few chairs. Gunther went over to the *Sicherheitsdienst* (Security Service) officer behind the desk. They talked in hushed tones while Alex, left standing between the driver and armed soldier, waited in abject fear.

Then Gunther beckoned him over to the desk. "*Der Herr Advokat* has a complaint," the *Kommandant* said to the SD officer.

Alex was dumbfounded. But Gunther went on: "He is complaining of destruction of property, and an antique clock is missing from his home."

The SD officer motioned to one of his underlings.

The soldier gave a brief command that Alex did not grasp, but it was clear that he had to follow this man.

The house had a large dining room built for entertaining, with an elevated podium in a corner. The room now looked like a warehouse. Alex first noticed the shoes, piled up to the ceiling on the podium— men's, women's, and children's shoes. Next to that were huge piles of clothing. Beyond those, he saw all sorts of household goods and smaller items of furniture, with rolled-up rugs lying on top. The soldier called him to the other side of the room. "*Uhren.*" He pointed at clocks of all shapes and sizes, stacked against the wall.

Alex briefly looked at each grandfather clock. A layer of dust indicated that they had been there for some time. Through the window in the doors, he could see into the glass-enclosed winter garden. In the past, it had given an added charm and sense of space to the room. The luxurious plants were gone now. Instead, he saw bicycles everywhere, piled on the floor and hanging from hooks. At a table, a man in German uniform was working on one of them. The air in the room was stifling. Nausea gripped him; he held on to a dresser, indicating to the soldier that he felt ill. But the man insisted that he take one of the clocks.

"No, it is not mine," Alex said.

"*Das gehört doch nur an Juden*" [But it only belongs to Jews] was the peevish answer.

Alex had only one thought: he needed to reach fresh air, and soon. He listened, sick at heart, to Gunther's offer of reparation. He knew that he had to find a way to refuse without giving Gunther an excuse for further harassment.

"I haven't seen any I would want to have, *Herr Kommandant*," Alex finally said. "The one we had was a family heirloom, you understand? My wife will be upset, but what is a clock, as long as we can stay alive through this war? I am sorry I complained. I have only one request. I'd like to walk to the gate to clear my head before we leave. I am not feeling well."

He walked slowly to the gate. He remembered a family visit, shortly before the war. The German menace had loomed darkly, and his hosts had been apprehensive. How naively trusting Nettie and he had been that a war would be unlikely or at the worst settled within months! Here, under the trees, the children had played, their voices ringing in the autumn air. They had gathered beech nuts, skipping among the fallen leaves. He'd grumbled later when the nuts were scattered on the floor of the car, pretending to be annoyed, but inwardly he'd enjoyed his role on such outings. He was grateful when Gunther let him out of the car near his office.

The place was strangely quiet. Work had become almost irrelevant. In one of the rooms, he found his secretary and one of his colleagues in hushed conversation.

Miss Kuiper produced a bag of dark wafer-like bread she had been able to bake on top of a small woodstove. "You look sick, Mr. van Vechtelen. This will do you good."

He began to tell her about his present life at the house, unburdening himself of the strain and fear he was living in.

She was comforting, understanding. "Remember, you can leave at the drop of a hat and come live with me and my parents. We don't have much, but we have a supply of potatoes and apples in the shed. We can last for a while. Don't wait till it's too late."

He thanked her, a lump in his throat. "I may have to accept someday, but for the time being I'll stay. After seeing our friends' house today... anyway, how much longer can it last?" Seeking refuge in his secretary's house would have been unthinkable even a few short months ago, but now it was heartening to consider the possibility.

With that thought in mind, it was with equanimity that Alex accepted Gunther's invitation that night to join him in his own office at home. The room appeared to be untouched since their last chess game.

Gunther began to set up the black pieces and, waiting for Alex to sit down and play, leaned back in his chair.

"You are *Judenfreundlich*," he said, as if accusing Alex of a hidden depravity.

Reluctantly, Alex sat across from him and pondered a possible reply. As silence would not do, he asked, "What makes you think I am partial to Jews?"

Gunther stood up and shouted, "I know that relatives of yours have been hiding Jews in this city!"

Now Alex became alert, but stayed calm. He had to proceed carefully and slowly in order to not aggravate him. He moved a pawn to start the game.

As he suspected, Gunther's only proof was the baby taken from Ada.

"But there were more," Gunther said in a threatening tone. "Others have been seen in her house."

Alex decided to appeal to Gunther's feelings. "I think this child was partly Aryan. I believe the mother had died. And because my aunt is a nurse..."

Gunther sat down. There was something mechanical about his outbursts. He, too, moved a pawn.

"Where did they take that family?" Alex, a white knight in his hand, tried to make it sound like indifferent curiosity. "To Westerbork?"

"They're not there anymore, *Herr Advokat*. All families with children were put on a transport to Auschwitz on September 4."

That was the day before *Dolle Dinsdag* [Mad Tuesday], when they'd thought the war was over in the Netherlands. Alex stared at him, aghast.

"Why! Why would the Germans even bother, now that this bloody war is practically lost?"

"This war is not over for you and your people, I can give you my word." Gunther spat out the words. There was nothing artificial about his anger this time. "We still have the means to win. If we don't, we will fight to the last man."

Alex weighed his response. "You have to forgive me, *Herr Kommandant*. I don't understand military strategies. I am only a lawyer and a stranger to armed combat. But to me, in my ignorance, it seems that your generals would want their troops defending German soil instead of keeping them here. It's your move."

"The Wehrmacht is useful here, *mein Herr Advokat*." There was a glint in his eyes. He blocked the threat to his queen presented by Alex's knight. "Just today, the Wehrmacht used 8,000 troops to surprise Rotterdam. This time they did it the right way. The city was surrounded before dawn, the bridges pulled up. They arrested 50,000 men to aid the German war effort out of an estimated 70,000 in the city."

The image was terrifying, but there was no doubt that the German was speaking the truth. Yet Alex decided to push on.

"But are men rounded up against their will reliable workers?" he challenged. "Certainly not healthy workers, considering the lack of food in the cities." He moved a bishop across the board.

Gunther gave him a cold stare. "Those who don't work will regret it. Anyway, they're easily replaced. This is only the beginning." He placed a pawn to stall the bishop's advance.

"There are no supplies of fuel or food, and the ports of Rotterdam and Amsterdam are destroyed now. Besides arresting people for forced labor, what is there to gain for the Wehrmacht or the SS?" Alex sacrificed one of his rooks.

Gunther's answer had an ominous logic of its own. "What do the Allies have to gain from fighting for this part of Holland? And despite what you think, *mein Herr Advokat*, we have secret stores of supplies, food, and arms, enough to last us for years."

In his surprise, Alex made an involuntary movement with his arm. It upset the board, and the pieces slid off. "This doesn't seem to be a propitious night for playing," he said, and bent down to retrieve the ones that had fallen on the floor. He put the pieces in their wooden box and closed the lid.

Gunther stood up. The shadow of a smile appeared on his face. "For you and me, *mein lieber Freund,* the war will last until the final victory of the Reich or its final destruction."

23

Screaming loudspeakers and the sound of gunfire woke him. It was still dark. From the street below came shouting in German and heavy banging on doors.

Steven shook Tony awake. It was expected, yet one was never prepared. What they had feared had come to The Hague: the mass roundup of men for forced labor.

Tony and Steven kept the weapons, ammunition, and radio receiver as well hidden as possible in the apartment. For those found with such items, immediate death would be the best option.

Tony peered through the window facing the dark street below. "They're everywhere," he said.

Steven couldn't see anything, but the sounds were unmistakable.

In that instant, the front door below crashed. Boots could be heard on the stairs a few floors below.

"The roof," Steven said. "It's the only way out."

They ran up to the top floor of the four-storied house and climbed through a window onto the flat roof. Steven looked around over the roofs of the buildings nearby. "There is no sense running anywhere when they're still looking inside." But he knew that it was only a matter of time till they'd think of searching the rooftops.

A gray dawn lightened the sky.

"*Schweinehunde, da herunter!*" [Bastards, down there!] The screaming was directed at them and came from the much higher roof of the railroad station across the street. In the mist, Steven could see the silhouettes of soldiers aiming their rifles at them. Bullets hit the flat roof and ricocheted off a chimney while they ran for cover.

Somewhere along the way they saw a small open window. They slipped inside to escape the bullets. In this building, too, boots marched up the stairs.

Their capture was swift.

They were taken to the railroad station to join a growing group of men. Steven and Tony stood with their backs against the wall, guarded by soldiers with their rifles pointed at them.

To his horror, Steven remembered that he still had his identity card in his pocket. It was not in his own name; in fact, it was a perfect facsimile of a real one. Being blacklisted by the Gestapo meant that he could not carry his own. Nonetheless, he worried about being traced through the card. *I have to get rid of it to protect Thea and my family*, he thought. He managed to bring the card behind his back and dropped it on the ground. Then he trampled it with his muddy shoes.

The gray light of the cold November day had turned to dusk before they were marched from Hollands Spoor railroad station across the city to a small theater near Staatsspoor station. The men stood waiting without food or drink the entire day, but now they were counted and given a piece of bread each.

It was early the next morning when they were marched to the inland port, where a Rhine barge was moored. The entire group was herded inside. Steven noticed there was water standing in the hull. He estimated it was at least six inches deep; it covered his ankles. More and more men were forced into limited space until there was standing room only.

The barge was hooked up to a tugboat and was moved only at night. During the five days and four nights that they were kept packed together below deck, they were required to urinate and defecate in the stagnant water. With practically no food or water, the need became sporadic.

There were incidents early on in their bizarre itinerary that took them from The Hague to Delft via Rotterdam, then through inland waters to Utrecht and Amsterdam. A screaming man fought his way up to the deck—a splash, then a few shots. Several times, someone slipped quietly up the ladder at night—a splash, a shot or two.

"That one got away," Steven whispered to Tony after one such incident. "I am going to get out of here. Are you with me?"

"I can't swim."

Tony's answer stunned him. "What? You're a merchant marine!"

"Hey, I'm a farm boy from the east. There wasn't much water where I grew up."

"I don't believe you. How can you graduate from merchant marine school when you can't even swim!"

"We were taught to stay *on* the water, remember? We have good shipbuilders in this country, Steven. Name one Dutch ship manned by Dutch mariners that went under in peacetime."

When Steven remained silent, he went on. "You take the plunge. I'll try to help by distracting that scum on deck."

"Forget it. Our chance will come." Steven stared ahead in the darkness. *We'll stick together*, he thought. His feet were numb now.

Finally they reached Lake IJssel. The waves made the vessel heave and roll. It was surprising how many felt the need to vomit despite an empty stomach. Amid the retching and moaning, Steven floated in and out of consciousness, starting awake when his body became slack.

At long last, they disembarked in Kampen, on the eastern side of the lake. The men were lined up, and an ice-cold November wind blew through their wet and dirty clothing.

Steven looked at the disheveled group marching ahead of him. *So that's how they do it*, he thought. *They make us despicable, dirty, weak. It's easier than to treat us like animals.*

He thought of the pink pigs in their scrubbed stalls back on the farm where he'd been hiding. *No, not like animals—much worse. No farmer treats his animals this way. No matter if we get sick and die, there are always more of us. We're not worth anything to them.*

A resolve formed, tightening all muscles in his body. Not me. They will never get me.

<h1 style="text-align:center">24</h1>

They were lying on the wooden floor of an attic in a former school. Tony and Steven managed to stay side by side. Two soldiers, rifles at the ready, patrolled from one side to the other.

The building was full of prisoners, and the toilets were overflowing. Steven had found out that the transport to Germany would take place at daybreak, by train this time.

He considered the possibilities. They could try to jump from the train, but the railroads were now run by the Wehrmacht. Would they have the chance?

The only possible exit from the attic was a small square window in the ceiling, approximately eight feet off the floor.

He whispered in Tony's ear that he would jump up, get hold of the window ledge, push it open, and hoist himself through onto the roof.

"You are nuts," was Tony's reply.

The moment arrived. The soldiers had turned their backs and were on their way to the other end of the attic. The challenge was to not make a sound. Steven jumped up and managed to grab the ledge. He pushed the window open and pulled himself through. Now he was standing on the sloping roof. He turned to help Tony up, but there was an unexpected problem: Tony was too short. Tony tried jumping, but he was just out of reach. He only had a few moments before the guards turned back.

Finally, Steven lay down on the roof and leaned through the window. It worked. He could reach Tony's hand, and he pulled him onto the roof. It was pitch dark. They slid down to the eavestrough and crouched on the eaves, bracing themselves with their feet partly in the eavestrough, waiting until daylight to orient themselves.

When daybreak finally came, they looked over the edge of the roof. The building appeared to be completely surrounded by armed soldiers.

"Let's go to the other side," Steven said. He walked in front. A building on the other side had an eavestrough about two yards lower. There was no time to hesitate. The only way to escape was to jump. Steven went first, hoping the noise would be minimal. He fell with a heavy thud against a chimney. A sharp pain in his chest stopped him for a second. Tony followed and doubled up in pain. As before, they followed the eavestrough to the other side of the building and looked down. It was a narrow alley, and there were no soldiers in sight.

Tony had come up behind him and said, "It's at least seven yards straight down."

"Looks like it. But there are no armed guards down there."

"I don't see a drainpipe. There's nothing to climb down on." Tony was holding his rib cage, still in pain.

Steven already knew the only way they could get down. But here, too, Tony would have more difficulty. The width of the alley was at least a yard.

Steven braced himself with his back against one wall and his feet pressed on the opposite wall. Scraping and shuffling his way down, he reached the ground, the clothes on his back in tatters. Looking up all the while, he guided Tony down, who at the end let go and fell like a brick.

At least they were now at ground level, but they found themselves in a courtyard. It was completely enclosed.

In a corner, they saw a cobbler's shop through a small window just above ground level. An old man, working on a worn pair of shoes, looked up and saw them. Steven was acutely aware of their shabby, unshaven appearance and wondered what reaction to expect. But the man bent over his work and began to tap away again on the worn shoe.

They noticed a fence on the other side. Tony began to climb. Now they were in a street leading to an intersection.

A troop of soldiers marched by in double file, singing. For a few moments, Steven and Tony fell in behind, unnoticed by the Germans. It was early; there were no citizens in the streets.

"At the first house, we'll ring the bell," Tony said. "The people in it could be on the wrong side, but what choice do we have?"

Steven agreed. "Two guys who have been lying in a sewer for five days will not escape detection for long."

When the door opened, two arms pulled them inside, as if they were expected. The door was hastily shut again. The warmth in a tiny living room enveloped them; a potbellied stove gave off the first heat they had felt in a long time.

"Take off your clothes," a middle-aged woman told them.

Her husband showed them where to wash and shave. Two teenage girls then served them large bowls of pea soup with bits of pork in it. They ate while they waited for their clothes to be washed.

When night fell, Steven and Tony slept on the floor while their clothes dried on wooden racks around the stove.

Steven awoke with a deep feeling of well-being and gratitude. He looked around the tiny room. A clock was ticking on the wall, and lace doilies covered the arms and backs of chairs.

Conditions in this part of the country seemed less desperate than in the western cities, but the family still did not have much. Simple folks, they were taking great risks by providing shelter for escapees.

Steven was not surprised when the father took them aside after a breakfast of apples and home-baked bread. "The whole town is swarming with German soldiers," the man said. "You have to leave now. This is all we can do for you. My daughters will help you get out of town. They still have bicycles—wooden tires, of course. After that, you'll be on your own."

Steven and Tony headed off on the bicycles with the daughters on the rear racks.

Where houses gave way to farmland, they dismounted and returned the bicycles to the girls. There was a brief, shy goodbye.

It was time to set out on the journey back, this time on foot.

During the entire trek southwest, they slept in haystacks in the daytime. Night was the time to push on. It was heartening to find that farmers never refused to help them along the way in this part of the country.

December was in its third week when they returned to The Hague. In their few weeks of absence, the conditions in the West had deteriorated. Deaths from starvation, particularly among the very young and old, had become commonplace.

With no gas or electricity, people had to become inventive to survive the uncommonly harsh winter. Trees were disappearing from parks and along the canals. Tram rails were pulled up to pry off the wooden ties between them. Inside houses, doorposts and doors were taken down for burning.

Then came shattering news from the front. A battle was raging in the Ardennes. On December 16, the Germans had started a massive offensive with the intent of pushing all the way west to Antwerp. American infantry divisions in the area were reported to suffer great losses.

The Germans had deployed much the same strategy in the First World War. Older people, who remembered, couldn't believe it. How could the same strategic ploy have taken the Americans by surprise?

So far, the Wehrmacht seemed to have made progress or, at the very least, to have succeeded at stalling the Allies' thrust toward Germany.

25

It was a recurrent dream. A large bowl of oatmeal boiled in milk was placed in front of her. Sugar lumps dotted the surface.

When she brought a spoonful to her mouth, it evaporated into thin air.

Riena woke up, her hand still in midair holding the imaginary spoon. She shook her head, thinking, *Why on earth would I hallucinate about a food I used to hate? There are so many delicious dishes I could've conjured up. I guess it means porridge is what my body needs, just as my mother said when I refused to eat it as a child.*

She gathered the blankets about her and got up. Rising early was not a problem; lying down had become uncomfortable and at times downright painful. It seemed as if every bone in her body made its presence known. She went over to the window.

Her room was on the third floor of the house. Early in the war, her parents had found it too dangerous. More than once, a sharp piece of shrapnel from antiaircraft shells had sliced through the tiled roof, one just missing her bed, but she had returned because she loved the view from the west-facing window. On clear days, she could see the North Sea in the distance. Sunset was a spiritual experience in that room.

She went to the washstand and splashed cold water on her body until her skin tingled. Then it was a matter of dressing quickly before the cold could get her in its grip again. Before going downstairs, she went into the part of the attic where the potatoes were kept, the one lifeline for the family. She carefully removed any sprouts because they would drain the food value. Then it was time to do a recount. She had made small piles, one for each day, to see how many more days she might be able to stretch the supply. Gradually those piles had become smaller as the end of the war seemed more distant. With the devastating news from the Ardennes in mind, she began her task of creating more, but smaller, daily rations of potatoes.

The cold was paralyzing, and a dull ache under her ribs reminded her that a meal was far off. The best way to deal with it, she found, was to keep moving. Holding on to the banister at the top of the stairs, she did ballet exercises. Keeping both legs straight, she swung one leg up, touched the toe with an outstretched hand, and counted one and two and three.

"I don't know where you find the energy," her mother said, huddled in a blanket near the potbellied stove. The cooking grille opening on top gave off a faint heat.

Midday was the time to go to the Central Kitchen. Large metal containers held a bluish-white liquid, with the odd grain floating in it here and there. Riena joined the silent queue of people waiting, pot and coupons in hand.

"Porridge today," the attendants told them. Young boys, each holding a spoon, were eagerly waiting to scrape out the empty containers. When one was set aside, they pounced on it.

The sound of an engine high in the sky made Riena look up. It was a clear day; she could see the silvery outline of a planelike object against the wintery blue of the sky.

"A V-1," said a little boy in front of her. "It's going to England."

A white-haired man beside him squinted behind his glasses. "That could be a V-2. It's not going to England. It's headed a bit too far south—probably meant for Antwerp, if it gets that far."

For a brief moment, the silent group came to life. Was it true that the machine did not need gasoline to fly? What kind of secret mixture propelled it? How many actually reached their target? Was it true that most crashed near the launching sites? And where were those launching sites, anyway?

Riena's mother examined the contents of the pot she had brought home. There was an expression of disgust on her face. "Look, Riena, there is dirt floating in it."

Riena set the table. They still used linen, plates, and cutlery, no matter how little food there was to be eaten. In the center, she put a large bottle of soy sauce, left over from supplies her mother had bought years ago. With a good serving of soy sauce in it, one could pretend it was soup they were eating.

They ate quickly, swallowing the tepid liquid with deliberation. Riena stared through the large dining room window. The shortage of fuel was so great that much of the shrubbery in the neighborhood had disappeared. Clouds had moved in. It had become a gray and foggy afternoon, but she could clearly see the platform of the railroad station and the soldiers guarding it, marching back and forth. One of them stopped and aimed. One shot, another shot. Riena's father noticed her preoccupation and stood beside her, watching. He pointed and said, "It's the coal."

A puff of black coal dust rose in the air. The soldier reloaded his rifle. Behind the pile of coals in the railroad yard, Riena noticed the head and shoulder of a shabbily dressed man. He was filling a bag but ducked again just in time.

"Poor fellow," her mother said. "God knows how people with small children manage. He needs it for his family, you can be sure of that."

It was the most they had shared in a long time.

26

"It's a surprise." Philip pulled her by the arm into the room. On the table was a small bottle of milk—regular, white, healthy-looking milk. Beside it was a package of oatmeal. A tin can covered the grille of a potbellied stove. Twigs were smoldering in the can. He poured the milk in a pan, placed it on top of the tin can, and stirred some oatmeal into the milk. "I'm making your dreams come true." He put a steaming bowl in front of her. "Have you had homemade sugar beet syrup? Have some."

It was a thin liquid that smelled faintly sweet. Riena poured some over the porridge.

"How's this for a Christmas party?" Philip watched her with a smile of expectation.

Riena eagerly took a spoonful. It was a powerfully rich taste. She took another spoonful but had trouble swallowing it.

Philip looked alarmed. "What is it? Is it not good?"

"It's very good." She took a third spoonful but gagged. "Oh Philip, it is too good. I can't. It just seems so awfully rich that it makes me feel sick."

"We'll finish it together." He looked disappointed, but he seemed to have no trouble eating it.

Suddenly a screeching sound made the house tremble.

"That V-2 launching pad is not far from here." Philip looked up, listening, spoon in hand. "You hope it falls right back on top of them, but that could also be the end of us."

She began rinsing the dishes. On the far end of the counter, she noticed a wide-open brown leather suitcase. Inside were a gray SS uniform and boots.

"What are you doing with the uniform?" She went over to close the suitcase, as it bothered her to see its contents exposed.

"There's been a request from Utrecht, closer to the frontlines. The uniform will probably be more useful there."

"How do you plan to get it there?" It seemed a daunting task, bicycling out that far in the cold. "Strong as I am, I don't think I can make it that far anymore."

He put his arms around her. "Of course you are not doing it alone. We are setting up a relay of couriers. You may be asked to participate, but only if you want to."

She turned her head to brush her lips against his. "You know I will do my part. I'll be glad to have that thing out of the house. Somehow that dead soldier still seems connected to it, wanting revenge."

"Don't worry, Riena. He had his revenge, a year ago. They never waste time with that."

"But you, Philip, did you pay?" She meant to tease him, but his expression forbade all further discussion.

Pulling away from her, he picked up her shoulder bag and went through her papers. "I want to be sure that everything is in place first," he said. "Oh, good, you finally have the correct number on your bicycle *Ausweis*."

She walked over, and he embraced her.

His fingers ran over her ribs under her sweater. "You've gotten so skinny, Riena." It was amazing how gentle those big hands could be.

Their lovemaking was tender, familiar now. They held each other close in the cold room. The warmth of his body made her drowsy. When she woke, he was watching her face with a peculiar look, as if something important was on his mind.

"I suppose we should talk about the future. About *our* future. I love you, Riena, and want us to be together for good."

In a flash, she saw him with her parents, her brother, her friends. It was impossible. She sat up.

"Oh, I see. I'm not good enough for you." For someone so inarticulate at times, he was lightning quick in reading her.

She got up and started to dress.

"Ah, sure. You just want to get laid. I am only good for that. Someday you'll do it for money."

She looked up.

His face had a mean scowl. The unexpectedness and vulgarity of his words stung.

She didn't want him to see her tears, so she turned around to look for her shoes. "That's not even worth contempt," she replied. She tossed her long hair over her shoulders.

In a flash he was there, grabbed her, and threw her on the bed. He moved too fast for her to know what happened. He held both her wrists in one hand, above her head on the pillow, and with the other pulled up her skirt. The weight of his body across her chest was suffocating.

The humiliation infuriated her. "If you do this, you will never, ever see me again."

He stayed motionless, but her wrists were hurting. In the silence, time had stopped. Then he let go and put his head on her shoulder.

"I don't even know if I could've gone through with it. You mean so much to me, Riena. You are magical to me, truly a whole different universe." He stroked her cheeks, wet with tears. "Don't leave me. Please, don't leave me."

They made love again, slowly, with an earnest intensity. All barriers were down in their own separate world, where she felt they belonged.

27

Alex unlocked the filing cabinet in his office and took out Nettie's jewelry box. He chose a gold bracelet he had once given her but had seldom seen her wear. She dressed simply, never the type to go about with dangling bracelets on her wrists. After some hesitation, he added a gold brooch set with three small diamonds that had once belonged to his mother and slipped both in his pocket. Going through his daughter's closet was more difficult. With a shock, he recognized blouses, skirts, and jackets. They brought memories so near that it caused him pain in the pit of his stomach. He took out a pair of leather hiking boots, once bought for a holiday in Switzerland. It was the first trip they had planned with the children after Pieter's birth.

These won't fit her anymore, he tried to assure himself. Yet some trace of her personality seemed to cling to them. He almost put them back but chided himself: *You sentimental fool.*

He met Ada down the street, the boots in a packsack on his back. A thin layer of snow covered the sidewalk.

"We picked a bad day." Alex looked at the leaden January sky. "Did you dress warmly enough?"

Ada wore a bonnet and scarf tied under her chin. A knitted shawl covered her shoulders over her coat. "Every day has been cold," she said, "and with so much snow! There is no use waiting."

It was her determination that had made him join her. It went against his sense of pride to go begging for food, even in return for gold and jewelry. The farmers near the cities did not accept money anymore. Food had become literally priceless.

Ada had finally won him over when she had said, "You can't go on like this, Alex! You look absolutely dreadful. What are you going to do for yourself? Everybody tries, at least!"

The walk to the farm was going to take at least two hours. He had once defended the owner in a property dispute and remembered one or two visits there in better times.

On the highway, they saw the endless procession of *hongerlopers* (hunger walkers). To Alex, it made the impression of a medieval painting. Older men, women, and children, often wrapped in rags, shuffled blankly along on the road. The lucky ones were pushing carts.

"Oh, look at these children." Ada wrapped her shawl around a small pale child sitting numb with cold in one of the carts.

Before Ada could take off her coat, Alex pulled her by the arm across the road, away from the crowd.

"There's nothing you can do, Ada. Keep walking. We have a long way to go."

"But don't you see? We're still privileged compared to them. My God, what is happening to the world?"

After a few minutes, she began again. "Why are they going north? People from Amsterdam and Haarlem have been there already. What'll be left? Amsterdam is worse than anything we've seen. At the hospital, so many people are dying so fast that they have to stack the bodies in the nave of the Zuiderkerk."

"Well, if they go south they head in the direction of Rotterdam. Is that any better?"

The flat polder land stretched before them. They had to lean into the icy northeast wind, and talking became impossible. Sudden snow squalls whipped across the flat land. Alex had to pay attention to the snow-covered path. It ran between ditches and narrow canals hidden under ice and snow.

Ada began to lag behind. He had to turn around to help her stay on her feet. When he tried to shelter her from the wind, she clung to him, panting. He almost lost his footing on the slope to a canal. She seemed to hang on for dear life, having forgotten now about her fellow man.

It was past midday when Alex saw the farm. The roof, partly thatched, partly red tiles, was shrouded in clouds of windblown snow. The gate was half-open, but he noticed a sign nailed to it: NO MORE FOOD AVAILABLE. Ada began to whimper, but Alex ignored her and the sign and went on to the entrance.

The kitchen was huge and dark. When Alex struggled to close the door, a voice bellowed, "Shut that door, dammit!" Klaas, his former client, had not changed. His square head and ice-cold green eyes expressed the same hard stubbornness, yet Alex sensed a mutual embarrassment between them. "Sit down! What're you waiting for?"

The farmer's wife placed a steaming bowl of bean soup in front of them. "Rest yourselves." She looked harried, but her voice was kind.

Looking around the warm kitchen, Alex noticed that they were not the only recipients of the farm's hospitality. People leaned against the wall, gulping down bowls of soup and warming their hands on the bowls.

Klaas followed his gaze. "I had to put that sign on the gate." He waved toward the kitchen door. "It's crazy. There's no end to it. At this rate, I won't have enough to keep feeding my own folks."

Negotiations were brief.

"Keep your jewelry, *mijnheer* van Vechtelen," said Klaas. "I would be ashamed to accept it. In peacetime, we're not worth a second look, but now everyone is knocking on our door. I have to keep a large enough supply to get my own family through the winter. Who's going to help me, huh?"

Alex took his wallet from his inside coat pocket and began to lay 100 guilder bills on the table, but the sight of them seemed to irritate his host.

"No, I don't want your guilders; what can I buy with that? It's not worth the dirt under my wooden shoes, although I remember you didn't come cheap." He chuckled. "Give me the boots. I can use them for my son. I'll give you 30 pounds of wheat for them. Take it or leave it. You have to get it milled yourself."

Alex remembered that his housekeeper knew of a mill where the wheat could be ground into flour. What choice did he have?

He was given an old children's sled to pull the 30-pound bag. With the wind at their back, it was easier now to walk, but Alex's legs were cramping with a dull ache originating from his lower back. From time to time he stopped to wait for Ada, who lagged farther and farther behind. Darkness had fallen when they reached the city. He then went ahead to Ada's apartment; she could find her way now.

Numb with cold and exhausted, he sat on the steps for 20 minutes or more, when he finally heard her limp along in the street. Curfew was at seven; she had just made it.

He opened the door for her, as her hands were too stiff. Inside, they had to find their way in the dark. Ada found a match to light what she called her "carbide" lamp. In its ghostly blue glow, he watched as she went to a wooden box in the corner, from which she pulled a pot, straw clinging to it. As she served them soup, she explained that the straw kept the temperature high enough to cook the vegetables. She was right. The soup was hot and the peas soft.

Wrapped in a blanket, he sat watching the light, waiting for dawn.

"Ada, you who believe in a loving God, don't you think He at least could have made this winter less cold?"

But there was no answer. Across from him, Ada had fallen asleep in her chair. Head tilted back, mouth fallen open, she looked like a corpse.

28

Riena adjusted the scales. In a book, she filled in the weight of the boy beside his height. It was clear that he would be in the third category. He was small for his age, but that worked against him. Shoulders bent, he looked at her with large dark eyes.

Marian stood at the door, letting in a few children at a time. Parents helped to undress the youngest children. In their underpants, or whatever passed for them, they were measured and weighed. Riena saw undergarments crudely fashioned out of horse blankets and draperies. Others were dressed in carefully mended, paper-thin underwear.

They were all proud parents who had been able to provide for their children in the past. Some had been well-off once; others had just scraped by. Now they were all desperate.

So many were waiting! Riena had to work fast, yet it was of the utmost importance to be accurate. She saw the anxiety in the eyes of the parents. One could not be swayed by it.

Of the four categories, only one could be admitted to the food program—those children at the very bottom of weight and health. The worst was explaining this to parents of children in the third category. Outside the door, she could hear a mother hysterically complaining to Marian. Couldn't anyone see that the child's bones were sticking out? Were they waiting until she was near death?

Unseen to them, Riena nodded in response. That's just how it was. There was simply not enough. Even those who were selected could be fed just once a week, sometimes twice.

At great risk of being hit by an Allied attack, a truck went over the Afsluitdijk, a dam that cuts off Lake IJssel from the ocean, to pick up a load of potatoes and cabbage in the northeast province of Groningen. The Interchurch Organization, together with the Medical Doctors' Group, had fought for permission from the German authorities to pass through the army checkpoints.

Riena helped set up the long tables in the school when mealtime came. Bowls and spoons were placed all along the tables. It was in the middle of the afternoon, and light streamed in through the large windows of the classroom. Children of various ages under 12 came in and sat down in total silence. Not one of them moved away from their own spot. Every time Riena was there, it struck her anew that they did not talk to each other. She had given up trying to chat with a child.

Then a sound arose from the children, a gradually increasing roar of excitement. She knew that the men pushing the cart with food had to be near, although they were not yet in sight. Looking out the window, she saw them turn the corner and come into view.

With the team, she worked fast to serve the children. Little ones ate as fast as the older ones. Each child had a solid portion of mashed potatoes and cabbage. There were no seconds. When they finished serving, the first ones were already scraping their bowls and licking their spoons.

The meal was over in a flash. Riena started collecting the bowls and spoons. She saw some of the other women scrape out the containers, standing around with bowls and spoons. It reminded her of the little boys at the Central Kitchen.

Marian brought her a plate. "Eat it," she commanded. "You deserve something."

It tasted like real food. It was amazing that mashed potatoes and cabbage, with a faint taste of gravy, could be such a heavenly culinary experience.

29

"I am so happy to hear your voice! We've been so worried!" Nettie's enthusiasm came through despite the crackling on the line.

Alex fought to stay calm. Emotion strangled his throat. He was using Henk van Waarden's line, aware that the connection could die any second. He couldn't think of anything to say. "How are you and the children?" He could barely speak.

"What? I couldn't hear you. What did you say? We hear it's terrible there, the hunger and all. Do you have anything to eat?"

He cleared his throat. "People are eating tulip bulbs now."

"Aren't you lucky to live in that region!"

Her humor was macabre. A wave of cold anger restored his speech. "Good, because we're eating the precious specimens you paid so much for," he said. "They're not exactly available in the grocery store, you know? But then again, I could go out to the bulb growers and barter away your jewelry."

"Oh, Alex, I am sorry. I guess we have no idea."

Was she crying? Did she hang up? The line was dead.

"What was that all about?" Henk had a puzzled look on his face.

Alex found it hard to explain. He felt sheepish when Henk burst out laughing, calling out, "Marian! You have to hear this!"

Marian smiled at Henk.

Alex noticed she was still an attractive woman, with a lovely smile. At the thought of Nettie, a lump formed in his throat. "Why do women still look so good, and we are scarecrows?" he asked.

"And cranky scarecrows at that," replied Marian. "Stay for lunch, Alex. We are having some of those tulip bulbs. You won't even notice them."

But Alex did. Although mixed in mashed potatoes, the slippery fragments stuck in his throat. He summoned his willpower to swallow them. His insides convulsed. Across from him, the two Van Waarden daughters were cleaning their plates without a word of complaint.

After the meal, he kissed Marian on the cheek and left.

On the way to his office, his bicycle chain broke and became entangled in the spokes. Without tools, all he could do was lift the back wheel and half carry the bicycle. His legs began to tremble with effort and fatigue.

At the *Mauer-muur* he threw the bicycle against the concrete wall in a moment of rage. *Let them have it, the bastards.*

Slowly he made his way through the city. It was cold and foggy, with some ice in the canal and snow still here and there. Along the water, garbage was piled up. Apparitions in dark clothing shuffled over the heaps, searching. Seagulls screeched, flying over his head.

In this black-and-white scene, soldiers were still patrolling, but they were an unfamiliar sight. They wore German uniforms but were generally short and stocky, with Mongolian features.

As he unlocked the door to his office building, he heard animated talking.

Miss Kuiper, her face beaming, opened the door to Alex's office. He was surprised to see everybody there.

"I picked it up for you. It finally came from the Swedish Red Cross," Miss Kuiper said. On his desk were a loaf of bread and a package of margarine.

He picked up the loaf and admired the size, color, and height. It was white bread with a golden crust, shining light brown on top.

"Everyone got one," she explained, showing her own.

"Come on, let's try it." Alex found a pocketknife in his desk.

They each carefully cut one slice from their own loaf and buttered it using their own package of foreign-looking margarine.

"Mm, it's good. It couldn't have come at a better time." There was an expression of bliss on Miss Kuiper's face.

Alex vaguely remembered hearing about this Red Cross project in October. It was now the end of February. It had taken four months to get through the Wehrmacht's objections and subsequently through the Allied command's demands for guarantees that only the civilian population would benefit.

But his secretary was right—it had come at the right time. Although the food itself was a one-time drop in an empty bucket, never to be repeated, the real impact went far beyond that.

"It is proof that there is still a world out there," Miss Kuiper said, as she looked at the unfamiliar Swedish lettering on the package of margarine. "And that there are people out there who care."

30

"It is an order from London to do it right by the railroad station," Tony said.

Marlise looked from Tony to Steven and then to Barthold. He looked surly.

"It's too close to the built-up area," Barthold said. "Too close to this house."

Marlise was grating sugar beets over a large bowl. "Why don't you tell them what the real problem is?"

Barthold squeezed the juice from the lump of grated sugar beets and poured it into a saucepan. It was a clear liquid that needed a long boil to turn into syrup. He continued, "I promised my father not to get involved while I was in his house. On that condition, he let Marlise and me in."

Steven's eyes narrowed, his jaw set. "Just don't tell him. Are you in or not?"

Marlise banged the grater unnecessarily hard on the bowl's rim to shake off the beet fragments. "With or without Barthold makes no difference," she said. "They'll search the houses here and find us anyway."

Barthold was pouring the last beet juice into the saucepan when his father came in. He gave the visitors a suspicious look and left again.

Marlise lit the twigs in the can on top of the stove.

Everybody had scrambled to find the old-fashioned potbellied stove. Barthold spooned some grated beet on a plate. Tony and Steven followed suit. The three ate silently.

Marlise shuddered. Men were different; they could eat stuff women wouldn't be able to get past their throats. She felt certain the lack of food affected them differently. Women could survive on less. *Somehow we are tougher*, she thought.

Steven cleaned his plate first. He tilted his chair back against the wall before he spoke. "We can go a few kilometers up the line, away from the station and residential area."

"You do it, then." Tony sounded annoyed. "I won't take that responsibility. That's not where it's intended. This is a direct order from London."

Why did men have to fight so much? It didn't seem to affect them or their friendship, though. Marlise, however, often felt the effect even hours later, her heart still pounding.

"I will take the responsibility then, alone. Everybody satisfied?" It was not really a question. Steven did not tolerate hesitation well.

"When you place the explosives, you need a lookout. I'll go with you as long as we keep my parents out of it," Barthold said. He sounded relieved, but Tony still had a frown on his face.

The night was bright with an almost full moon. Marlise had reached a state of acute wakefulness. She pictured the men out there in the stark moonlight, amid contrasting brightness and shadow. Her heart was pounding, and her eyes seemed to be stretched wide open.

It was still, except for a sudden burst of gunfire now and then in the distance. Each burst startled her, and she clenched her fists in front of her chest. Midnight went by; the troop transport was expected to pass shortly after.

At long last, she heard the faint chugging of a locomotive. It came closer. Nearby, it slowed down, probably near the railroad station. Then the chugging sped up again.

She stood up in the darkness and waited an eternity. Then she heard the explosion. Right after, a hissing sound rose and sounds of crashing. She unlocked her bedroom window according to plan. Tony was the first to climb in. Sometime after came Steven and Barthold. Barthold stood still, listening.

On the stairs were footsteps—his father running upstairs. "How dare you? You gave me your word!" Barthold's father stumbled over his words in anger. "How dare you endanger your mother and your fiancée? I want you all out of this house by tomorrow morning!"

Marlise sat by the window until daybreak. It came early; spring was just a few weeks away. In the twilight, the birds' singing seemed unnaturally loud. Thoughts tumbled incoherently. It was impossible to focus on a plan.

Her lookout post was on the third floor. Dawn broke to a clear day. In the distant dune landscape, almost bare now of trees and shrubs, the first rays of sunlight revealed helmeted soldiers everywhere, combing the terrain methodically. How long till they'd search the streets and houses?

Breathless with fear, she ran downstairs. Barthold's father was grim faced; his mother was crying.

"You can't send them out now! Look outside!" Marlise pleaded.

There was a hand on Marlise's shoulder. Behind her stood Tony. With a quiet air of authority, he said, "You better stay out of this." He turned to Barthold's father. "I want to speak with you alone, sir. I think we'll come to an understanding very quickly." She heard a clear hint of threat in his voice.

After no more than five minutes, Tony and Barthold's father came out of the room, talking calmly to each other. The older man seemed subdued.

Soon everyone was busy readying hiding places for four people in the house. Marlise was the only one unarmed, so the others insisted that she be separate from them.

Outside, people were clustering in the street, angry. They were afraid of retaliation. Why these acts of sabotage now? What difference could they make? Would civilians pay for it?

31

The house trembled with the power of the explosions. Alex stumbled downstairs, holding on to the banister. What was happening? Because there had been no electricity for some months and his batteries had run out, he had not been able to use the radio. He saw Gunther rushing through the hallway and front door.

Despite Alex's fear, he felt hope. Was this the beginning of the fighting after all? He foresaw days of sheer terror and destruction, but it was the price of freedom. The explosions stopped as suddenly as they had begun. There was the sound of airplanes high in the sky.

Alex opened the front door. People were running about. Someone pointed in a northeasterly direction, and he saw smoke and dust billowing from the city. He began to walk toward it, a still-unnamed dread oppressing his chest. A man carrying a blood-spattered child ran in the opposite direction.

"It's Bezuidenhout," the man shouted in passing. "We need everything—sheets, blankets, everything!"

But Alex kept going, compelled by that inner dread. And then, abruptly, he entered the scene. As far as he could see, city blocks were reduced to rubble. He was pushed roughly aside by men carrying a stretcher. Here and there, people were prodding and pulling at the rubble. Some people were just walking around, dazed.

Still he went on, but a weakness in his legs made him stumble. The world began to spin. He sat down on the ground and shut his eyes, his head on his knees.

A familiar voice called out, "Hey, Alex, are you all right?" Henk van Waarden bent down to look him over. "If you are, go over to that young boy and stay with him until they come with a stretcher."

Alex tried to comfort the child, who cried incessantly for his mother and father. After what seemed like hours, Henk came back to check on him.

"He is going to be all right," Henk said. "Can you help carry him? We are short of stretchers and man power. What were you doing here, anyway?"

"My secretary and her family live around here." Alex made a vague gesture. The flattened neighborhood was unrecognizable. "I was planning to move in with them."

"Believe me, they didn't have time to feel a thing." Henk patted him on the back. He glanced down at the child and lowered his voice. "It's a miracle we are finding anybody alive. He's the only one in his family."

Alex mustered the composure to be professional, concentrated on the immediate need. "What happened?" he asked.

Henk looked away. "The what is not difficult. They bombed the city. But the *why*! Why did they do it? The people will be enraged. That won't do us any good, Alex."

Before the day was over, Alex had already seen much of the rage and bitterness. The most reasonable explanation he heard was that the Allied bombers had attempted to hit the V-2 launching site—an attempt that went horribly wrong.

He dragged himself home. At the top of the first flight of stairs, he noticed a light under his office door. He threw it open. Gunther was leaning against the filing cabinet in the flickering light of a candle. He pointed at the calendar on top of it.

"March 3, *mein Herr Advokat*. A dark day for the citizens of The Hague."

Alex sat down, unable to answer. It had been March when Gunther had first set foot in his house.

As if reading his mind, Gunther said, "We had our first chess game, *Herr Advokat*, almost a year ago. Let us play in commemoration of that first game." He began to set up the black pieces.

Alex tried to concentrate, but he made a disastrous move early in the game. It was a quick win for Gunther. When he stood up to retire, Alex detected a flicker of triumph on his face.

Alone, Alex sat staring at the candle until the flame died in a puddle of melted wax. He felt empty of thought and the will to move.

It took a few weeks before he heard the details. The final death count of the bombardment stood at 500. According to the official explanation from London, it was "a navigational error by the Royal Air Force."

By then, he'd heard rumors of a new wave of terror. After all this, did he still have to go into hiding? Why would they bother killing off small groups of the resistance when they had a war on their hands, a war that by all accounts was lost?

He had to find out. Perhaps there was still time.

On Karin's old bicycle, much too small for him, he struggled along to the Van Waardens'. He straightened up and walked in.

He had never seen Henk nervous before. Henk seemed to be one of those lucky people with a deep conviction of their valued role in the world, but now his hands were trembling as he threw bundles of papers in the fireplace.

"The news is bad, Alex. God knows how far this is going to go."

"You mean the attempt on Rauter's life is true?"

"But it wasn't, Alex. They couldn't have known who was in that car. It was incredibly bad luck, a roll of the dice."

"What happened, exactly?"

" A resistance group had set out to ambush a Wehrmacht vehicle between Arnhem and Apeldoorn with the sole intent of 'requisitioning' it."

"Oh, I see. And what comes by is the SS *Polizeiführer* himself, Rauter."

"Right, in an open BMW. Mind you, he is not alone. To our men's surprise, there is violent gunfire."

"But it didn't kill him."

"No, but the fight went on until the car was completely wrecked. When our men withdrew, they didn't know that inside that car riddled with bullet holes was a seriously wounded German officer named H. A. Rauter, with the impressive title of *Generalkommissar für das Sicherheitswesen und Höhere SS- und Polizeiführer* [Commissioner-General of Security Forces and Higher SS and Police Leader]. It seems unbelievable, but only in real life do you make blunders like that."

"Good Lord! Somebody as important as Rauter will not go unrevenged."

"Exactly. More than 400 people who were arrested on suspicion of being resistance workers have been executed—117 in the area of the ambush."

Alex began to feel a familiar cramping in his stomach.

"That's not all, Alex. In the south and east of the country, they have killed all the resistance supporters who were imprisoned, just before the Allies move in. Why? Because they're vicious and vindictive. There's no other explanation."

"Are you saying that we are next?"

"They have started in the West already. The latest execution was on March 12 in Amsterdam. They shot 36 men, making them stand on a garbage heap."

This last detail suddenly made the retelling all too vivid. Alex shut his eyes but could not blot out the vision.

"They forced people to watch, Alex. Afterward, someone ran out and covered the bodies with a Dutch flag."

"Was there anyone we know?"

"No. But we are sure now that Leo was arrested some time ago. What happened to him is not certain. One rumor is that he was shot on the spot. Another source tells me that he was sent off to Mauthausen like the other agents, which is hardly better. My guess is that he was among the 400 executed. Schöngarth, *Kommandant* of the *Sicherheitspolizei* and SD, is responsible for all of this. He gave the orders."

Alex stared at the flames. "Are you getting ready to leave?"

Henk threw another bundle of papers in the hearth and poked

the fire. "It's not easy to find a place for a family at this point," he replied. "People already don't have enough to take care of their own. Besides, I have my work." He glanced at the clock. "I don't know why Riena is not here yet. She was part of a relay today to Utrecht."

They heard a door slam, running steps. The door burst open. Marian's mouth was twisted in a scream.

"Henk!" she yelled. "Look outside! They are taking Riena's father away!"

They were just in time to see him between two armed soldiers before he was pushed in a military police car. Pale-faced, staring blindly ahead, he looked like a sleepwalker.

32

Riena stood before a desk between two soldiers. Behind the desk sat a uniformed man, looking her over with a cold stare behind his glasses. On the desk, cut open, was a brown suitcase with a gray uniform in it. She ignored the questions of the man behind the desk. Nobody would know she understood German.

The man stood up, leaning forward, and started shouting. Being screamed at touched a source of fury in her. She tossed her hair back and shouted back in Dutch, "I don't know what you're saying!"

He hit her so hard in the face that she staggered. With an effort she stood erect again, her face stinging. He drew his hand back again, but in an instinctive movement of protection, she hit his arm with the back of her forearm, hard. In the clash, his glasses went flying.

Her arms were grabbed and twisted back by the two soldiers beside her. The man behind the desk was shouting obscenities at his subordinates, demanding they help him look for the glasses. They responded in unison, "*Jawohl, Herr Kommandant.*"

She was tied to a chair now, as more uniformed men had appeared. At one point, a blindfold was tied around her head. The incessant shouting continued. She felt a great need to use the toilet.

Then they left her for what seemed like hours. Finally, she heard a door open. Her blindfold was removed, and a tall man in civilian clothing stood before her. He started talking to her in a gentle tone, in Dutch. "How did you get yourself in this mess?"

They must have believed it, then, that she didn't understand German. She felt grateful when he untied her. She rubbed her wrists. "I have to use the toilet, badly," is all she said.

"Of course they'll let you use the toilet. And they'll send you home right away, you and your father."

A shock ran through her body. She saw its reflection in his eyes. Don't give yourself away so much, she told herself.

"Yes, you and your father," he continued. "It's up to you. First, you have to answer a few straightforward questions. You're not surprised that they wonder what you're doing with an SS uniform, are you?"

She remained silent, thinking to herself, *Don't let him trap you. He's a traitor, a contemptible, despicable collaborator.*

"Look, I want to help you. I have a daughter your age. I'll tell them that you didn't know what was in the suitcase. Give me a chance." He seemed nervous, his kindness an act. "All I want you to answer is, who sent you on this mission? You're not working for the Wehrmacht; nobody knew you in that office. We know that your *Ausweis* is false."

He seemed to realize that the "we" had given him away. His tone changed. "You are a stupid, foolish girl to get involved with those Underground criminals. They used you, and you let them. You can save your own skin and your father's by answering one simple question. Where did you get this suitcase? Who gave it to you?"

Fear took hold of her mind and body to the point she was unable to feel anything else. Was it better to say something? Anything? "A man in the street handed it to me," she finally said. "Of course, I didn't know him. If what you say is true, do you think I'd be allowed to know anybody?"

He sighed. "You're not making this easy. One last question. Where were you taking it?"

This was easy. The truth was that she was to take it 20 miles out of town on a country road and meet a relay she'd never seen before. She told him this, adding, "And that was yesterday."

His expression showed he didn't believe the truth either. He kicked his chair aside. "All right. You're stubborn as well as stupid.

We'll get the truth out of your father. He's being interrogated right now. We'll see if he thinks your friends are worth protecting."

He waited to see her reaction. What did he expect? That she would say, "My father doesn't know anything" or "Please leave him alone"? That would give them a great opening and probably wouldn't help her father. Her mind was racing, but she didn't speak.

He opened the door, and the brutes were back.

Now she was stretched out on an elevated bench. Nauseated with fear and revulsion, she felt herself being strapped onto it. And then she saw what one of them had in his hand. They were heating a long needle, like a knitting needle. Terror dried her throat.

Rough hands grabbed her head, pulling it sideways. Other hands pulled her hair back. She felt something sharp touch her ear, and a searing pain obliterated everything. She fell into a darkness in which she heard an animal lowing in pain. Then there was white light and no pain, but she could see with a sort of awareness that was beyond her body. She knew her body was there, also that the German torturers were there, and what they were doing to it, but she couldn't feel her body.

The darkness enveloped her again, and she became conscious that the animal's lowing had come from her own throat. She could smell her own blood and burnt flesh, and pain took hold of her, overpowering all other sensation. Words said began to have meaning; they were obscenities because she had wet herself.

"She'll talk after this, the bitch. We'll give her a night to think it over before we do the other side." She was dragged down a hallway and thrown on the floor of a bare cell. She was lying on her side, her hands pressed hard on her head. The pain was less unbearable if she kept strong pressure on that side.

Chills began to run down her spine. She knew that it was the beginning of a fever; her palms were hot. Thoughts became external, burning images.

It was morning when the door was unlocked. She hadn't moved. It was important to maintain pressure on her head, even though she was trembling with fever.

Boots sounded on the floor, then stood still beside her. *"Das ist doch Scheiße hier!* This is the stupidest thing I've ever seen. We catch one and you try to kill her before she talks? Get her looked after, today! Understood?"

There was no hesitation. *"Jawohl, Herr Kommandant."*

Hands were oh so gentle, washing her, dressing her in a spotless gown, placing her in a bed with white sheets. Tender care surrounded her. When she tried to speak, the nurses placed a finger on their lips and nodded at the door. When the door was opened, she got a glimpse of a soldier standing guard.

33

"So you are Philip." The man in the white coat turned to him.

"Doctor van Waarden, I have to see her. I was told you might help me."

"I don't know how much I can do for you. You have to remember that she is guarded at all times. I myself went in only once." Henk took off his white coat. "The doctors and nurses here are doing what they can for her."

"At least tell me how she is."

"We've brought the fever down with aspirin, and we are fighting the infection with sulfa drugs. The nurses give her painkillers. The infection is still festering. It will take time." He handed the coat to Philip. "I'll show you the way. They can't keep her here much longer. Those lowest of the low want her just well enough to start again."

Philip had to take off his sweater to fit his broad shoulders into the white coat. He couldn't button it up.

Henk looked at him. "What have you got there? A revolver? Don't even think about it. They've taken over the whole floor."

"But what about outside when they take her back? There must be a chance then."

Henk hesitated. He shook his head. "I promise you one thing: I will let you know when she is taken out of here." He opened the door. "I'll show you the way."

Philip followed him. He took note of the guards posted on that floor. At the entrance to Riena's room stood one single guard. Philip opened the door with an air of authority.

At first, he didn't recognize her. Her head was completely bandaged as if swathed in a huge gauze turban. Her face seemed strangely denuded, her eyes darker. The pupils in her clear green irises were large. Her dark, wideset, boyish eyebrows gave her an air of childlike vulnerability. A hard lump formed in his throat. When he bent over her, a finger on his lips, tears began to form and slide down her cheeks. Her mouth formed a silent "Philip." He held her hand, speechless. His chest seemed constricted in pain.

She sat up and whispered close to his face, "They never asked for the *Ausweis*. They just grabbed the bicycle. Then they saw the suitcase and ripped it open. It was just a stupid, stupid thing. All for that bicycle."

"Shh. You did everything right. Everything." He stroked her cheek.

"Philip, I am so afraid." Tears flowed again. "Promise not to let them take me back there." She heaved a long, shuddering sigh. "I don't think I can do it again."

"I promise." He stood up. "Don't be afraid. I'll be back."

He couldn't let the guards get suspicious. Besides, he had things to do. He wanted to get a good grasp of the layout of the hospital.

When the time came, he had practically lived there for several days. The Germans had taken all possible precautions. No one could get near her that morning. He had taken his position on the balcony above and to the right of the front entrance. As he expected, that was the route they took, the shortest way across the grounds. It was a group of at least 20 armed soldiers. Then he saw her with her bandaged head, walking slowly in the center. From time to time she stood still.

Cold hate steeled his resolve. He took aim at the grotesque white head and fired.

For a few seconds, she disappeared from sight. Then he caught a glimpse of her, lying on the ground. There was pandemonium around her. Looking for cover, the men dropped helter-skelter on their stomachs, aiming their rifles anywhere.

He went inside, threw the rifle under a bed, and walked calmly out a back door. A strange tranquility had come over him. He had died inside.

34

Alex slowly walked along the sandy slope, picking up a twig here and there. He carried a canvas bag to collect them. He sat down in the moist sand. Fatigue seemed to overcome him more often now. He clutched a handful of gritty sand. It felt warm. Wildflowers had pushed through the humid soil. High up in the blue sky, swallows were darting around.

Back home, Ada greeted him with a smile. "The sun feels warm here on the balcony, out of the wind. Come and look, I dried these crocus bulbs."

The small grayish-white clumps were neatly aligned on the brick edge. She picked them up one by one and put them in a handheld coffee mill. He watched as she turned the handle patiently. Now and then she emptied the mill in a bowl and refilled it with the tiny bulbs. The sun warmed his back.

Ada, too, lived in this stagnant pool of desperate waiting. Yet somehow she was capable of continuing to bustle about.

After Riena's arrest, Alex had expected the worst, every day, every night. Henk, tight-lipped, maintained that no one knew anything— only that her father had been sent home with a bundle of her clothes.

But the last week in March had brought new hope. The Canadians had begun to fight in the east of the country, moving to the west and north. Nettie and the children were now in liberated territory, behind the front line.

When he heard in mid-April that Arnhem and Apeldoorn were in Allied hands, he had decided to move out. Surely, the Canadians would reach the west coast any day now. He'd be safer in Ada's small apartment for those few days and nights, away from Gunther. But the front had stalled in the center of the country. What could the reason be? It was true that the Germans had flooded sections of low-lying land to make defense easier. They had threatened to destroy the Afsluitdijk to let ocean water into Lake IJsel from the north.

Troops certainly seemed to be around in great numbers. They were no longer the Mongolian-looking occupation troops, which rumor had it were Georgians kept under guard on the island of Texel, just off the northern tip of western Holland.

"Maybe I should go back to the house." He watched Ada as she formed small flat cookies using dough made with crocus flour and water. "The Americans are in Germany. The Russians are going to take Berlin soon. What are all these local German troops going to do?"

Ada baked the cookies on top of the emergency stove and offered him a small plateful.

"It's strange," he continued, as Ada watched him munch. "We all expected that the Allied invasion would come from the west and that we'd be the first to be liberated. Instead, it's going from east to west, from the direction of Germany."

Ada took a bite. Screaming, she ran to the sink to spit it out. "How can you eat this stuff? It tastes horrible!" She turned to look at him. "I think it's poisonous! Don't eat it."

Smiling, he showed her his empty plate. "I'm learning."

The banging on the door came at night. As soon as Alex heard it, he knew. He had expected it for a very long time. On his way out, he got a glimpse of Ada praying.

The night was long. Somewhere in the prison, he heard a scuffle and screaming. He sat on the cot and tried to think of Nettie and the children. Instead, he had visions of the men in Amsterdam standing on a garbage heap in front of a firing squad.

He was blinded with fear when they took him out of the cell the next morning. They had taken his belt; he hung on to his trousers.

Dimly he recognized the office and a familiar voice.

"*Guten Morgen, mein Herr Advokat.*" Gunther motioned to the soldiers to leave him alone with Alex. He pointed at a chair and offered him a cigarette. "*Kaffee*? It is only ersatz, naturally."

Alex began to sip the hot liquid. His blood was still pumping hard, but his brain had cleared. He sat up straight.

Gunther leaned forward, staring at him with his pale-gray eyes as he spoke. "Regretfully, I must say that these are very unfortunate circumstances for you, *mein Herr Advokat.*"

Alex took another sip and waited.

"I once made an offer, *Herr Advokat*. I think you remember."

Alex nodded. His mind began to work feverishly. Was there a way out for him? This negotiation was familiar terrain. If only he could stay focused.

"Your situation is less favorable now, *Herr Advokat*. Perhaps you want to reconsider."

"Maybe your situation has become somewhat less favorable, too, *Herr Kommandant.*"

Gunther waved this remark away as inconsequential. "Here and now, I have the power of life and death. Do you want to see your wife and children again?"

Alex did not reply. It was important to wait for the offer and counteroffer. What would be expected of him?

"You will be allowed to return home. You will be treated as my friend again." Alex flinched at the word "again," but Gunther continued, "All I want is your cooperation."

Alex thought feverishly of an avenue out, but somewhere in his subconscious the decision was made. It just was not quite clear yet. How much cooperation did Gunther want and for how long? How much could he stall until the Canadians' arrival?

Goddamn him. Goddamn Gunther Blechmann.

He heard his own voice: "I want to see my wife and children again."

35

He was running as fast as he could, breathless. It was too late to go around on the road, so he ran on the railroad tracks to the station. It was the familiar one of his childhood days, in the town where he grew up.

It was of crucial importance to catch the train. Already he could hear its approach.

Now he was on the platform, still trying to run, but his feet would not move forward. He saw the train pass by and then, behind a window, the tear-streaked face of Karin. Her lips formed "Daddy," and a profound sadness pervaded everything.

He struggled to reach the moving train, but a massive dark figure held him back, pressing something against his throat.

Gagging, he opened his eyes. Over his bed loomed a hulking shape, now releasing the pressure on his throat.

"Well, Alex, you want to call your German friends for help? Go right ahead. I am ready for them too."

Alex felt the cold barrel of a handgun against his cheek. His eyes adjusted to the almost complete darkness, but he recognized Philip mostly by his deep voice."Philip. Keep it down," he whispered. "They're not my friends." He looked at the French doors opening to the balcony. One seemed slightly ajar. "Are you alone?"

Philip ignored the question, but he lowered his voice. "I know what you are. I've always suspected you. You son of a bitch, with your connections in the jail. Connections, hah! You've always played both sides, haven't you?" There was cold hatred in his voice.

Alex sat up. "You've got it absolutely wrong! I've done all I could, always."

"The arrests this past week—it can only be you. No one else had all that information."

There was a moment of silence. A silence more damning than any reply, but Alex couldn't cross the line of utter betrayal. When he finally spoke, it was as a man resigned to death. "I am a virtual prisoner here. All I have done is stall for time. Every day I hope it's the moment of liberation. The Canadian troops are only a few hundred kilometers away. This last week, I admit, I've tried to save my life by giving them bits of information—piecemeal, day by day, as little as I could."

"Without warning anybody?"

Alex saw a glimmer of a possibility to barter for his life. "How could I try to reach anyone?" he said. "I haven't seen anybody until now. You think I could be seen with any of you? I figured people had time to move after my—" He hesitated. Did they know about his arrest? Admitting he'd been arrested and freed would be enough for this maniac to pull the trigger.

"Aha! They picked you up and you sold us out. You deserve to die."

Suddenly Philip grabbed him around the neck with both hands, pressing his thumbs on his larynx. "When? When did this happen?"

Alex struggled, choking, trying to pull the man's hands off his throat. "Only a week ago. I swear. At my aunt's place." He gagged, but the pressure was released enough for him to utter: "Let go. I'll tell you everything."

So that was it. They hadn't known because Alex had moved in with Ada. Philip relaxed his grip. It was his turn to remain silent. He heaved a long sigh and said, "I came here to kill you with my bare hands. The gun is just for the Germans, in case they interrupt. But first I'm going to force out of you all the information you gave them."

Alex stared at the dark outline of Philip's head and shoulders. The man was strong, but he had a chance if he played his cards very carefully. "I told you—I give as little as I can. I'll cooperate with you. I can be your double agent if that's what you want to call it."

"Double agent," Philip mimicked. "Speak up, or do I have to choke you again?"

"Do you all still meet in the old clubhouse in the park near Scheveningen? Near the canal?" He could sense the shock that went through Philip's body.

Putting the revolver under his jacket and backing away, Philip said, "For now, I'll let you go. I have work to do. But I'll be back. Be sure of that. If it's the last thing I do, I will find you and make you pay."

Alex saw him slip through the French doors. When he went to shut them, he couldn't detect any movement in the yard below.

The rest of the night he sat on his bed with his blankets drawn around his shoulders. There would be no more sleep now. Blankly, he stared at the glass doors, waiting for dawn. He felt irrevocably stuck as if in a sticky web, waiting to be wrapped up and devoured. But who would do the wrapping? The Gestapo or his resistance friends?

His days had become an aimless wandering in the streets. Sometimes he joined people in line if the rumor reached him that a bakery had a supply of bread. For hours he would wait with his food coupons in hand, often to find that the supply had run out before his turn came.

Today he was one of the lucky ones. For the next few days, he would allow himself two slices twice a day. He was cutting a greenish-looking slice off the small hard loaf when he heard a knock on the door. On the doorstep stood a young woman, holding a little boy by the hand.

"I am Martha Schönhart," she said. "May I come in?"

Flinching at the German last name (What could this be? Was she sent by Gunther?), he led her into the front room. Gunther had taken over the dining room as his office; much of the furniture had been stacked in the front room where they had received visitors in the past. He found a seat for her and sat on a table across from her.

"You know my parents, the Driessens," she began. "You and your wife were in the same tennis club. They sent me here because they think you can help me."

He looked at her, waiting. She had that rare combination of honey-blonde hair and dark-brown eyes, with the pink complexion of a blonde. He had a vague recollection of her parents, both accomplished tennis players and part of their widening prewar social circle, in a former life, now like a barely remembered dream.

"Mr. van Vechtelen, please help me. I married a German. My parents were against it—I mean, my getting involved with a German."

"How did you get yourself..."

"My mother had friends in Germany before the war. Then one day a young soldier, their son, came to our door. Hans Schönhart, now my husband."

Alex stood up. "I am in no position to help anybody."

"Please, Mr. van Vechtelen! Haven't you ever been in love? I was crazy. We both were head over heels! It was 1941, and I was 17. Politically, he was not on Hitler's side."

"That's what he told you." Alex began to feel uneasy. She looked at him with moist brown eyes, wringing her hands. Despite himself, he sat down to listen as in the old days when a client would come to see him, in a time when he could afford to be charmed by a face like this.

"No, really, he wasn't," she insisted. "But still, we had terrible fights about it at home. I got pregnant, and he married me. He got this small furnished row house for me in Voorburg."

"I suppose it had belonged to Jews," Alex said.

She nodded. "I know. My parents took me back when he left for the *Ostfront*. But all the neighbors know." She pulled the little boy onto her lap. He leaned his head against his mother's shoulder, looking sideways at Alex from under long dark lashes.

"I am afraid, Mr. van Vechtelen. What is going to happen to me and my son after the liberation?"

"What about your husband? You and your boy are German. Have you heard from him since your son was born?"

"No, but he promised to come back here for me. If he's alive..."

Tears reddened her eyes. "Do you think he wanted to fight at the *Ostfront*?" She kissed the top of the little boy's head.

"Mr. van Vechtelen, the *Ortskommandant* told me that wives and fiancées are allowed to go with the troops when they go back home. I don't want to go to Germany! I have no place to go. I'll wait for him here. I want to stay with my parents; they love my little boy. But we have been warned that things can get quite ugly for us."

Alex rubbed his forehead. It was difficult to imagine reality after the occupation "You are right," he said. "You may need protection. The people are angry and will take it out on people like you. But in truth, I am not the right person to come to for help. For the moment, we have no idea how long it will be before we are liberated." He pulled a pencil from his pocket and wrote Ada's address on a scrap of paper. "Talk to her," he said as he handed her the address. "She loves little children. She may be able to find you a place when the time comes—someplace where you can wait till things have settled down."

When he closed the front door behind her, he was deep in thought, struggling with the image of a new reality. The people's suppressed rage would be unleashed on anyone who had associated with the oppressor.

The liberation, so desired for such a long time, would be ugly for some people. And he could be one of them.

36

"Come on, we have to move! We have to get there on time!" Philip gasped for breath. Tony caught up, pedaling furiously against the strong northwest wind.

It was close to curfew time, but the sun was still high in the sky. It would not set until after eight, but they could not afford to wait for darkness.

They stayed off the road as much as possible, even if it meant pushing the bicycles. The wooded area near Scheveningen had been depleted of vegetation, but some remaining underbrush and larger trees still offered limited protection.

When the old wooden clubhouse came into view they stopped, completely out of breath. It stood in an open, abandoned sports field. The uncut grass was knee-high. There was no sound except the chirping of birds and the whirring of insects. No human being was in sight.

"Let's leave the bicycles here. We'll circle around through the underbrush to the back and then crawl through the grass," Tony said. "The distance across is shorter there."

They proceeded slowly, listening at every step.

After circling halfway around, Tony got down in the grass and started crawling forward on his elbows, keeping his body low to the ground. Philip followed his example.

It was when Tony rose on the steps to the back door of the clubhouse that they heard the first shot. Inside, a group of men was alarmed by the sound. Stock-still, a few rifles pointed; the men stared at Tony and Philip bursting in through the door. There was little time for explanation. Philip grabbed a rifle and peered through the windows. He listened to Tony's brief instructions.

Why were other cell members so early? The meeting had been set for around nine, after sunset. Who changed the time? It had been impossible to warn everybody. Philip had spent the day in a frantic effort to do just that. Were there others still to come?

"We have to take the risk," he heard Tony say. "The shots came from this way, so go out the other side one by one, crawl to the bushes, and start running to the canal. We have to hope that they have not had time to surround us. We'll cover you. Hide in the old barge in the canal; you know which one."

From time to time Philip fired a random shot just to see where the Germans were in the underbrush.

Tony had guessed right. The Germans had come from the east and now were moving south and north to surround the open field. The setting sun would hamper a clear view of the clubhouse windows for the Germans and would thus make the west the best direction to escape from the clubhouse.

Tony supervised their flight at the front of the building, which had a veranda toward the west, until the last of their men disappeared from view.

"They're gone. It's our turn," Tony said as he came in through the front door.

Just then a salvo of shots hit the northwest corner of the building.

Philip swung around. He fired at a group of soldiers coming from that direction. The Germans got down into attack position, but one was pulled back by a comrade, obviously hit.

"This way!" Tony pointed at a southeast-facing window. They pushed it open and dropped in the grass. Hunkering down, each still with a rifle, they scanned the open field. Fortunately, it was high enough to offer some cover.

Philip knew that their only hope was that the Germans would concentrate on the clubhouse.

"You go ahead." Philip motioned. "I'll keep shooting and will come later."

Leaving his rifle behind, Tony began to move stealthily through the grass. Philip crawled under the low veranda with both rifles and fired a shot in a northerly direction, followed immediately with a shot in a southerly direction.

There was return fire from both directions but, incredibly, no other attempt to cross the field, as far as Philip could see. Most likely, the Germans believed that a large group of armed men was still inside the clubhouse.

The temptation was great just to stay put and kill, over and over. He wished he'd brought hand grenades.

Then he saw Tony standing up at the edge of the woods, both fists urging him on. The fool! As if Philip's life had any meaning left except revenge.

Philip signed to Tony to get down and crawled through the grass until he reached the woods.

They were almost at the canal when they ran into the patrol. Although they only had their handguns now, they reached the water, running and shooting. Philip jumped in and turned to see Tony follow, but Tony ran along the edge, a black silhouette in the now orange light. Philip heard a shot, and Tony crumpled to the ground.

Philip sank underwater. He touched the sandy bottom and kicked off his shoes. He struggled out of his jacket and noticed a bloody streak on his arm, dissolving in the water. He felt nothing but the icy cold. When he came up to gulp air, he was met with a hail of bullets. Hit in the shoulder, he sank again. Something in him took over, a blind determination to reach the other side, out of the numbing cold and into the air to breathe. He swam underwater as long as he could and, stumbling onto his feet, emerged where it became shallower. Shocks reverberated through his body when he was hit again and again. Coughing, he pulled himself onto dry land and lost consciousness.

When he opened his eyes, he was lying on his back, shirtless. Sharp stabs of pain in his chest brought back the memory. Around him stood a group of men in SS uniform, looking down at him.

"*Er kommt wieder zu sich*," [He's regaining consciousness] one of them said, bending down. With a hand movement, he commanded, "*Nur zu!* He doesn't have much time."

In the dim light of dusk, Philip saw on each side of him a soldier with a rifle aiming down, a sharp point touching his chest. Alternately, they shouted questions at him, but not in German like the first speaker—this he recognized as Flemish. Philip coughed. He wanted to wipe the warm blood off his face, but someone was standing on his hand. Their goal was clear—they wanted to know where the others were hiding. His mind cursed them: damn you, damn all of you, German and Belgian SS-ers.

They turned the bayonets in his chest. His body twisted in pain; his jaw locked.

The command was shouted again: "*Scheisse!* Try again! We're going to lose him!"

They lifted the bayonets and prodded a new spot on his chest. "Speak! Where are they?"

The sharp pain, the intolerable twist in his skin. He closed his eyes; his limbs cramped. But in his mind was a triumphant hate: You can't make me do anything, say anything. I'll be free.

The German shouted in disgust. "*Verdammter Schweinehund!* He is dying. Let's go."

Drifting in and out of consciousness, he was lying under a starry night sky when he heard voices. A flashlight shone on him, briefly.

"Hey! We found him. He's in bad shape but still alive. He's lost a lot of blood. We've got to get him to a hospital, fast."

37

"So you were back home and I didn't know! Not until I was told by that young mother, Martha Schönhart." Ada sounded indignant. "The grief it has given me not to know anything!"

They were walking along the Zeestraat toward his office.

Alex knew nobody would be working now, so it was easier to talk there. Besides, he didn't want Gunther or his cronies to see her in his house. "I didn't get in touch with anybody." Alex unlocked the door.

"But how about me? It was cruel not to let me know."

How could he share the shame and guilt? He slowly walked up the stairs and opened the door to his office.

"What did they do to you, Alex? What did they want?"

He remained silent. How could Ada understand the entanglements a man like him could get himself into? He lacked her simple convictions and unshakable faith. For her, everything was straightforward.

"What made them let you go?" She finally asked the question he feared.

"It was one of the *Kommandant*'s ploys. I guess he believes I can be more useful to him alive." He was hoping this would satisfy her.

"You mean when the Canadians get here?"

He was thankful to her for finding a satisfactory explanation, letting him off the hook. He nodded. "I suppose."

She stood leaning against the south-facing window where the sun could warm her back, watching him pace the floor. He couldn't see the expression on her face in the shade.

His mind was in a whirl. How much did she suspect? What would her Christian conscience tell her to do?

"Alex, you have to come with me to the interdenominational service in the Grote Kerk tonight. Don't shake your head. You shouldn't miss it. It's this incredibly brave young minister who is in hiding himself. He is on the Gestapo's blacklist. It's at seven o'clock."

"But that will run past curfew time."

"Nobody cares about that now. Anyway, there'll be safety in numbers. You'll be surprised." She moved away from the window.

He tried to read her face. Her eyes, so similar to his, seemed brightened by compassion and love, but her lips were compressed in a determined line. He needed her loyalty, more than ever.

The ancient church was already packed when they arrived, but they found seats side by side on folding chairs placed in the aisles. In his damp coat, Alex felt the chill in the building. Sleet and rain streaked the windows, but it did not prevent the crowds from coming. Huddled in coats and scarves, people kept coming through the doors.

During the next half hour, more and more streamed in, filling all seats, and standing or kneeling on the gray stone slabs covering centuries-old graves. Looking down, Alex noticed the Latin lettering and date on the ledger stone under his chair. Beneath him rested the decaying bones of a burgher and his beloved wife. He couldn't decipher the date; it was eroded by countless feet over hundreds of years.

No sound came from the poorly dressed, famished crowd, but Alex sensed an emotion-laden atmosphere in the church—or was it just him? The mood seemed to match the sober, imposing interior, with high arches reaching to the sky. Once built in Gothic style when the Catholic Church was all-powerful, it had been denuded of its statues and opulent decoration in the time of the Reformation, during the war for independence from Catholic Spain.

As a schoolchild, he'd had to learn the details of that brutal war, which lasted 80 years. People born, living, and dying, never to see peace in their lifetimes—unimaginable in these days of blitzkrieg, he thought. Would there be any of us left if our war lasted even half that time?

Yet in their own way, these forebears were capable of monstrous cruelty toward others and horrible acts of vandalism, such as the plunder and destruction in this church. They'd been unable to ravage the building itself, and now its starkness emphasized the grandeur of its architecture.

Alex felt a new connection to the suffering in ages gone by. With compassion, almost fondness, he thought of people as well-intentioned, busy as ants, running around to tend to their daily business. And yet they seemed just as tiny and vulnerable as those insects, blind to the forces that could crush them.

He asked himself, *We see people from those distant days as cruel, foolish, and ignorant, but are we any better now?*

There was a disturbance near the pulpit. A group of young men suddenly arrayed themselves around its circular staircase and surveyed the crowd. This was different from any service Alex remembered. The tension rose when the minister climbed the steps. He was a young, haggard man, dark haired but very pale. His voice was amazingly strong and rich for his thin frame. It filled the church.

The overall impression of his sermon, if one could call it that, was anger. For the first time, Alex heard a description of the concentration camps in Germany, recently discovered by the Americans. The minister shook his fists at the evil brought about by Hitler and his followers. He also did not exonerate anyone who assisted or obeyed in the execution of their crimes, or even anyone who did nothing, who simply had stood by.

He finished by praying, "For those who lost, or still risk, their lives fighting this scourge."

A young man beside Alex fell on his knees, tears streaming down his face.

Alex felt his own chest racked by dry sobs. He had trouble breathing. Ada put her hand on his arm, her face serene.

The minister descended and left, surrounded by the young men protecting him. Shortly afterward the church began to empty, in complete and total silence.

The sky had cleared. Thin clouds passed over the moon. It was a long walk to Ada's apartment.

Alex broke the silence. "Did you notice he never used the words forgiveness or redemption? Or hell or heaven? He seemed so focused on the here and now."

"That's why I thought you would like him. He is a secular type."

"You're right. He was fascinating."

They turned into a narrow street. An intense fatigue came over him. He stopped on a corner, pretending to listen for the sound of soldiers' boots.

"The people kneeling to pray were Catholic, I suppose," he mused. "Sometimes I think Catholics are enviable. They confess their sins to a priest, a mere mortal, do penance, and are forgiven."

She looked up at him, the moonlight blanching her face. "But Alex, we all will be forgiven if we are sincere in our remorse."

He waited. "Is it so simple, Ada?"

Her eyes were dark orbits in a white face as she spoke. "If we repent and believe in Christ."

He walked on. It sounded like an ancient formula, alien to him now.

38

The first wave of low-flying bombers they saw through the French doors took them by surprise. Barthold ran outside to see the planes pass over the rooftops and remaining trees. A hatch in the bottom was open; men in unfamiliar uniforms were clearly visible, watching and waving.

"The food drops!" Barthold roared. He ran inside and grabbed a tablecloth to wave back. Marlise followed with two tea towels, performing a sort of dance on the lawn.

She had never seen anything more beautiful. It was like a sea of gratitude toward those men up in the sky, in communion with the enthusiasm of the men above. With each it was a magical though fleeting bond. Wave after wave flew over. Everywhere around her she could hear the screams of delight from houses and streets. Where did all these people suddenly come from? She put her arms around Barthold's mother, who seemed overcome with emotion. His father shouted till his voice cracked, running back and forth.

The British radio had announced that an agreement had been reached to drop food supplies behind the lines for the people in western Holland. It was planned for the day before, a rainy April 28, but nobody was surprised when nothing happened. The Germans were very much visible, and skepticism had long ago clouded any hope of relief. But the next day was sunny, and the mere presence of the planes changed everything.

It didn't matter that it would take weeks before any of the food would reach local distribution centers. The prospect of food, although sorely needed, was not the real reason for all this joy today. What mattered was that Allied planes could come in just like that, flying so low that the Dutch could see the faces of their liberators, and the Germans wouldn't shoot—the first contact with the outside world now that the antiaircraft guns along the coast were silent.

"Now we can believe," said Marlise. "At last it is over. The Germans must have realized it, and they know that we know!"

Barthold came back from a run down the street. "One of them unloaded on a field nearby," he said. "He wasn't supposed to; it probably was just a humane gesture, a hello to us down here. I am going over."

His mother walked slowly back to the house. "Remember in the beginning when the British fighter planes were being shot down? That was the last time I could see the faces of those men, flying low over the treetops," she said.

Walking beside her, her husband took her hand. "Spitfires and Hurricanes—great planes, but no match for the Germans then," he replied. "You know, that's just about five years ago. Who could have imagined it would last that long?"

Marlise recalled the image of small flaming airplanes plummeting from the sky. The thought of the human beings inside would tear her up each time. She recoiled from the direction her mind was taking. Since then, so many lives had been lost, many seemingly as senselessly. She listened to the shouts and laughter around her and straightened her shoulders as if shaking off a burden. After all, this was a happy day, a day of immense relief.

Barthold was back within an hour, looking thoughtful.

Marlise prodded, "What is it? Was there no food?"

"There was—a container stuck in a tree—but armed Germans were holding the people back. A boy ran out to look at it, just a kid, and they shot at him."

"It was not a designated area," his father said. He sat down heavily, tired from the emotion. "You know, the Germans may be getting nervous. I suppose we have to play by their rules until the war is officially over."

39

Marlise felt her anxiety rising. She had been separated from Barthold in the seething mass of people, and it had become obvious she would not be able to find him.

Barthold had grown up near this city, but Marlise was not familiar with the network of narrow, winding streets leading to Haarlem's Grote Markt, the central market square. She could not budge from her place in the crowd anyway, and she was too small to see over the shoulders of the people around her.

Barthold had become restless. It was too difficult to sit still and wait any longer. Nothing seemed to be happening. Marlise had agreed to walk with him to the center of the city to see action, if any.

Clearly, they were not unique in their desire to find out what was going on. The previous week had seen a succession of amazing events. The Italians had killed Mussolini on April 28. Two days later, Hitler had died by suicide. And on May 4, the Germans had officially surrendered.

Yet nothing seemed changed. Armed Germans still patrolled the streets. They still requisitioned bicycles from people who had been hiding them in cellars and attics these last years. It was optimistic and foolish to bring them out now when any kind of wheels would be at a premium.

She had never seen so many people packed together with barely any room to move. It was a fight to get through, which is how she and Barthold had been forced apart. She decided not to panic and to stay put until the crowd started to thin out. Ahead, she noticed recently built scaffolding in front of the old Vleeshal (Meat Hall) with its distinctive stepped gable. Only the top platform of the scaffold was visible to her. She now saw a woman being pushed by a uniformed man onto the platform. She recognized the man's uniform as that of a Dutch marine. A feeling of nausea gripped her.

There was no jeering or applauding. The crowd simply stared as the marine began to shave the woman's head. He bent down to dip a brush and painted two strokes on her head, forming an orange cross. What struck Marlise was that during all this time the woman had a silly sort of smile on her face, as if to placate the crowd.

A group of men pushed another woman forward, the next victim. Marlise turned around. Behind her, she made out the voice of a woman reciting poetry. This woman, too, stood on a raised podium on the other side of the square. Only her face and shoulders were visible.

Then Marlise heard the sound of heavy vehicles. From behind the majestic Great Church, a number of German tanks appeared. While they rumbled past the square, the men turned their heads in the direction of the spectacle. Without slowing down, the tanks disappeared on a road opposite.

Marlise saw the crowd disperse somewhat and struggled through to the church. She felt weak; it was good to sit down. Leaning her back against the wall, she put her forehead on her knees and shut her eyes to stop the spinning of the world around her.

Sometime later, she heard Barthold's voice. He sat down beside her, a flyer in his hand. "This is the first time I can openly carry around an illegal newspaper." He showed it to her.

"Did you see the marine with those women over there?" She nodded toward the scaffolding. "It made me sick—such an ugly scene in such a beautiful place. Look at those great old buildings around the square and this beautiful cathedral. It's sacrilege."

Barthold grinned. "These grand old buildings have seen people in stocks or drawn and quartered. You want me to tell you what the Spanish did here in 1573?"

Marlise stood up. "No, please, spare me. I don't know how I'll make it back as is. Tell me what's in the paper. Why are the Canadians not here?"

"Apparently there is an agreement about the organization of the surrender. There are between 116,000 and 120,000 German troops here, north of the rivers in western Holland, and they are armed to the teeth. Another problem is the land mines. It will take a long time to locate those."

They walked hand in hand, slowly.

"Does it mention us, the resistance?" Marlise asked.

"We are the Domestic Armed Forces now, my dear woman. They are taking prisoners—collaborators and such, and some Germans who deserve special attention but may be overlooked by the Canadians."

The inner city was behind them now. Her feet were hurting in her worn shoes. They rested, sitting on the narrow handrail of a bridge. Marlise stared over her shoulder at the dark-green water.

Barthold was still scanning the paper and said, "They warn about overzealousness. People will go overboard in their anger. Innocent people may be interned."

"Innocent as those women today?"

"Were they innocent? Were they punished too harshly? Their hair will grow back. After all, they associated with Germans."

"They probably did it just to have something to eat."

He stood in front of her, smiling. "You'll be a good lawyer for the downtrodden. And you constantly remind me why I love you. Come on, I'll give you a ride on my back. Two blocks."

She giggled, hanging on to his shoulders like a child.

Exhausted, they arrived back home to find Steven visiting with Barthold's parents. He'd made a perilous journey from The Hague. He had seen many Germans but no sign of the liberators. He'd hoped to find Thea at her parents' home nearby, but he was told that she was still in Amsterdam.

40

Thea moved with the crowd through the Kalverstraat to the Dam. From what she had heard, a communal singing event would take place in front of the Royal Palace. The Canadians were expected today, any time now, and what better way to welcome them?

Thea loved to sing and looked forward to the joyous event. The last few days had been a roller coaster of hope and disappointment. Food distribution had stopped altogether. The last time she'd been in a line for bread, she'd witnessed ugly scenes of hysteria and despair. The mood in the city today was one of tense expectation. Officially the war was over, but where were the liberators?

The tension was caused by this uncertainty and the nervousness of the Germans. The citizens were restless, and armed German soldiers still patrolled the streets. A few shooting incidents caused civilian casualties. The hoisting of the orange flag on the Royal Palace on the Dam was met with a hail of bullets.

But that day, the seventh of May, the word somehow had spread that peace and liberation would be celebrated with music and singing, and the surge toward the Dam and Damrak was unstoppable. Thea ran along, carried away by the crowd's enthusiasm for what they thought would be a happy occasion.

She laughed when she saw an old-fashioned street organ in the middle of Dam Square, wheeled out to help greet the Canadians. It was a symbol of happier days.

Suddenly the excitement of the crowd reached a fever pitch. A British reconnaissance of two jeeps and a couple of armored cars arrived on the scene. The people went wild, surging toward the vehicles, cheering. She couldn't see the vehicles, but the joyous shouting from that part of the square was unmistakable. Then she saw something else.

Open German trucks full of soldiers moved through the sea of people. It was easier to see them because the crowd made way for them. These soldiers were still holding rifles. Was that for their own protection? Thea wondered what went through their heads underneath those helmets. Were they angry, relieved, afraid?

To the left of the Royal Palace, she saw men in German uniform standing on the roof of the Groote Club, a men's social club. It had been occupied by the *Kriegsmarine* for years now.

Small groups of armed men of the Domestic Armed Forces supervised the scene. Their task was to disarm groups of German military found among the civilians and to take them under guard to the Royal Palace.

She heard jeering in that direction and then, suddenly, a shot. Bystanders told her that a couple of German officers had been pulled off their bicycles by the former resistance fighters. Did the Germans resist?

A split second later bedlam started. *Rat-a-tat-tat*! It sounded like machine-gun fire.

A man beside her yelled, "It's coming from the Groote Club! Run for cover!"

Before being carried away by the screaming crowd, Thea looked at the building to the left of the Royal Palace. She could see Germans behind the windows, on the balcony, and on the roof.

"Hold on to me," the stranger beside her commanded when she lost her footing.

Some people tried to find shelter behind the street organ. Overturned baby carriages and scattered shoes were left on the ground, among the dead and wounded.

When the crowd thinned, she leaned on the ledge of a store window, still stunned and speechless. Then she saw, coming toward her, men from the Domestic Armed Forces, nurses, and scouts in uniform waving flags fashioned out of white bedsheets. They were heading back to the Dam, and she joined them.

For the rest of her life, she would retain the image of Dam Square at that moment, but it would take years before the enormity of what had happened would hit her. All she was capable of now was to look around and register. Except for the victims, the square was devoid of people, but their possessions littered the ground—bicycles, shoes, hats, and baby carriages. The poignancy of the baby carriages. The bizarre sight of the street organ, still standing. Using it as a cover, a young doctor examined one of the wounded.

Despite the sound of occasional gunfire, they began to work. First, the wounded were carried off on makeshift litters and a handcart. There were many.

Afterward, in the hospital, she heard the final count: 120 wounded and 22 dead. One German soldier was among the dead, shot by the Domestic Armed Forces. By then the British reconnaissance had left, the same way they had come.

Slowly, painfully, Thea climbed the stairs to her room under the roof and kicked off her shoes. Eyes closed, she dropped on the bed. The images of the day were burned into the insides of her eyelids.

When she woke it was dark. She saw Steven's head and shoulders silhouetted against the tiny window. She blinked. Was she hallucinating? But he turned to her, looking comfortingly real.

"Good, you're awake!"

She jumped up and put her face against his chest, where his heart was beating. He put his arms around her, holding her tight, swaying gently back and forth. "It's all right now; everything is going to be fine," he said softly. "I'm taking you home."

In the street stood a German military vehicle, but in it were two young men in Domestic Armed Forces uniform. Thea was surprised that Steven had arrived with members of that group, but she didn't ask questions. She was only too glad to go home and leave the city where the ugly scene had played out.

41

There now was no food at all in the city. Pets, either eaten or starved to death, had disappeared.

Alex trudged through the streets. It was warmer than inside, as long as he kept to the sunny side of the street. Peace was officially three days old, but there were few signs of it. Ahead of him, he saw three children on the sidewalk: a boy of about 11 holding two small children by the hand. Just when Alex passed them, the older child crumpled to the ground, his thin face blue. A small group of passersby gathered when he knelt down by the child. Helpless, Alex looked up at the faces around him. He saw the same helplessness and angry frustration.

Finally, a door opened and a woman called out, "I have nothing for them, but bring them in."

Alex walked home. The anger lingered when he began to search through the rooms that Gunther and his entourage had occupied. The booty was three bottles of gin and a small tin of sausages. Taking the tin, he went up the stairs. He meant to go to his bedroom, his last refuge, but he was too tired to go up a second flight of stairs, so he turned to enter his study.

The door was ajar. Pushing it open, he was startled by the scene in front of him. Sitting at the round coffee table, in his old place, was Gunther. But there was something unfamiliar about his appearance.

Coming closer, Alex saw what it was. Gunther was wearing the uniform of a private in the Wehrmacht instead of his SS officer's uniform and boots.

Alex sat down across from him and placed the tin of sausages on the chessboard. Gunther's face looked haggard, with a twitch around the mouth.

"When are the Canadians coming?" he asked.

Alex collected his thoughts. Caution had become too ingrained a habit. "The people in the streets say maybe tomorrow," he said finally. For the first time, he could read emotion on that face—disbelief, irritation, fear.

"We are in this together, *mein Herr Advokat*. You have to play the game my way, or we both perish. I won't hesitate to tell your friends that you betrayed them."

So it had come to this. There was no way out. Gunther had him cornered.

"As a lawyer, you must be aware that the Dutch government-in-exile has reinstated the death penalty for traitors," Gunther continued.

The man did his homework. He always had known which buttons to push.

"I have no inside information about the arrival of the Canadians," Alex replied. "I haven't seen or talked to anyone who has. I myself think they'll be here tomorrow at the earliest." One couldn't be too careful.

The twitch around Gunther's mouth returned. "Twenty-four hours is enough time. If we play our game right, we'll both live with our wives and children again."

Alex took a deep breath. "What is my part in your game, *Herr Kommandant*?"

Gunther's pale eyes narrowed in a near smile. "We fought a long battle, *mein Herr Advokat*. But in the end, I won."

Alex looked down at the table. He waited.

"I am the only person who knows that you betrayed your comrades. But your secret is safe with me."

Alex's muscles tensed, but he did not speak.

"*Natürlich*, I want something in return. I want you to hide me until the Canadians arrive. They will oversee our withdrawal. And, as you know, many of our troops are here. When the time is right, I want you to help me join a unit of our Wehrmacht, identity unknown."

Alex rubbed his forehead. It was important to think clearly.

But Gunther was impatient. His fist hit the glass tabletop. "You have no choice! Your secret is safe with me as long as my secret is safe with you."

Still, Alex was silent.

Gunther reached for something under his tunic. It was a revolver. "Of course, I could kill you if you refuse. What is the better course? Do you want to see your wife and children again? Think about it. They should be here soon."

"How can I hide you? This house will be searched by people who know."

Gunther's face contorted in anger. "Of course not here! Where do you go every day?"

Alex stood up with a sigh. "Fine. I'll take you to my office. We have an agreement, *mein Herr Kommandant*. Our battle is over. We'll call it a draw."

Gunther made him walk in front, staying about 20 feet behind. The streets were practically deserted. Alex was aware of Gunther's eyes trained on him, probably so Gunther could kill him if he bolted.

After unlocking the front door to his building, Alex waited inside. He heard a discreet knock on the door and let Gunther in.

"Put your revolver on this ledge, *Herr Kommandant*. Enlisted men do not carry officers' handguns."

Gunther hesitated.

Alex went up the first step. "Don't worry about me. I never touch those things."

Gunther placed the weapon on the ledge and followed him up the dark stairs.

A new energy took hold of Alex's body. He unlocked the door to his office and breathlessly waited for Gunther, half expecting the man to hesitate and go for his gun. But he didn't; he came straight upstairs and walked through the door.

He showed Gunther around his office, pointing out the couch and private toilet (after all, the man expected a longer stay), and left. After locking the door, he pushed a filing cabinet in front of it just to make sure Gunther would stay put.

He bounded down the stairs. The sight of the revolver filled him with disgust, but he picked it up anyway. He gingerly pushed it into his pants pocket and made certain the front door was locked behind him.

A sense of urgency overtook him as he rushed over to the newly occupied headquarters of the Domestic Armed Forces, one hand over his pocket to steady the gun. He could not permit himself any hesitation.

The young men inside wore makeshift, ill-fitting uniforms. He didn't recognize any one of them, but they needed little explanation when he handed them the keys and the handgun. The name and reputation of *Kommandant* Gunther Blechmann sparked their immediate interest.

When he left, his step was light. A burden had lifted off his shoulders. He felt drunk with gratification.

Back home he sat down at his desk and began a letter to Nettie.

42

Unfamiliar music filled the large rooms. Steven looked at the pairs dancing energetically to the beat. The young officers swung and twirled the girls around in a dance he didn't recognize. Jitterbugging, they called it. He saw Marlise being tossed in the air. Her flaming copper curls flew up around her laughing face.

He looked over at Barthold, but Barthold shrugged. He had explained to Steven that the colonel had taken Marlise under his wing, whatever that meant. He called her "my little redhead." According to Barthold, it provided Marlise a degree of protection from unabashed pursuit by the younger officers, who glowed with robust health in comparison to him.

It was a party offered to the local resistance members by the officers of the Canadian regiment, and Steven had come up for the occasion after picking up Thea at her parents' place. He looked around for her and spotted her dancing in a close embrace with a soldier who seemed to be leaning on her, keeping his eyes tightly closed. She looked flushed but not pleased. Steven went over and tapped the man on his shoulder. He let go and staggered over to the bar.

Steven was a good dancer and easily moved to the new rhythm. He maneuvered Thea through the crowd to the French doors that opened to the terrace. There, too, people were dancing and drinking in the moonlight.

The last few days had seemed unreal. To the boundless joy of the population, the Canadian troops had arrived on the eighth of May, and the exodus of German troops had begun. It was a strange, almost comical sight to see a lone Canadian in a tank at the head of an endless column of disheveled German soldiers.

A bell announced that a supper buffet had been laid in the dining room. Double doors were opened to let in the guests.

There was an ah of surprise and admiration from the Dutch guests. Among arrangements of flowers and candles, the tables bore food they had not seen in a long time. Various breads and cakes, canned hams, and fruits seemed like a sumptuous repast. Since the Canadians had arrived, the local population had been subsisting gratefully on their main food aid, hard but nourishing hardtack—army biscuits—which were definitely nothing like the colorful display they saw now. Their hosts were smiling with pleasure.

Steven and Thea were invited to sit down at a table with some young officers. Steven looked over their heads at the wall, at the skull and crossbones of the SS Totenkopf Regiment that had occupied the house. It was still everywhere, marking walls and doors.

Thea followed his gaze. One of the officers, who introduced himself as Ted, seemed to be struck by her expression. He bent over to her. "The Germans were here before us and made sure we know it."

"We know only too well," Thea responded. "But I was in this house, I mean, before the war. I knew the people who lived here."

He looked thoughtful. "It must be hard for all of you; first the German army occupies your country, and now we're here."

She stared at him, astonished. "Steven, did you hear that? I can't begin to explain. My English is not good enough."

Steven grinned at Ted, a crooked grin. "God knows we're happy to see you here, Ted. It's been a long wait." It was true, words could not describe how they felt. These men seemed to come from a different planet.

A soldier came over to Ted, saluted, and tapped him on the shoulder.

"Excuse me, something has come up." Ted put down his napkin and left.

Steven and Thea were dancing slowly on the terrace under the fragrant May sky, his arms snugly around her to keep her warm.

"Why don't we go home?" she whispered. "I could fall asleep standing up."

In the opening of the French doors stood Ted, a drink in his hand.

"You're back," Thea called out with a wave.

Looking grave, he walked toward them. "Two of my men picked up a couple of girls in the village. They backed up in their vehicle to turn on the village road. A land mine, just off the road—one of the girls is dead, the other..." He shook his head and emptied his glass.

"The men?" Steven asked.

The Canadian shrugged. "They were lucky, both sitting in front."

Where the land mines were hidden was anyone's guess. All day long, explosions could be heard from the direction of the dunes. Removal would take a very long time.

A small party wound up at Barthold's. His parents welcomed Ted and his friends, who seemed grateful to come to a home where English was readily understood and spoken.

Without prompting, one of them sat down behind the piano, and around it they all began to sing, "Oh give me land, lots of land... don't fence me in!" Their nostalgia showed.

Aware of the empty stores, some of the Canadians would later return from such visits with gifts of chocolate, cans of corned beef, or cigarettes.

One night they talked of a discovery nearby—large underground stores of food, weapons, and ammunition kept hidden by the German army. During the last couple of years the Germans had been sitting on these vast supplies, waiting for what? What were they holding out for?

In that part of Holland, the death count due to starvation had been determined to have reached at least 15,000.

43

Riding in an open jeep was a new experience. Marlise was in the back seat with Barthold; Steven sat in front, beside Ted. The wind was so strong that it felt as if Ted was driving at breakneck speed. The road to The Hague was rough with neglect, but there was no traffic to worry about. Marlise had tied a scarf around her head, but the wind loosened it and blew it away. In the golden glow of the cool spring evening, she clung close to Barthold for warmth. Ted had offered to give them a lift, and Barthold went along for the ride. She saw Barthold lean forward to hear what Ted and Steven were discussing.

Ted stopped the jeep, his expression grave in the orange rays of the setting sun. Without the noise of motor and wind, a vast stillness surrounded them. He gestured west toward the dunes. "That's where we found the mass graves today," he said. "So far, we located five of them, and at least 400 bodies—shot in the head. They are mostly young people, and apparently some have been dead only a few weeks. One was a woman. There were no clothes, nothing to identify them. Well, I suppose except their teeth. They will have to use dental records."

Marlise shivered. She knew they all were thinking the same thoughts. Did the Germans kill them here, or were they already dead and brought here? Did they make the naked victims dig their own graves? She tried to blot out the image of their comrades, facing death in the windswept bleakness of the dunes in winter. "How lonely they must have felt," she whispered.

Steven's jaw was set. Barthold stared into the landscape of the dunes beyond the road, frowning. Neither one spoke.

Marlise slipped her hand in Barthold's and left it there the rest of the way. Closing her eyes, she forced away the intolerable images. Would life ever be normal again? The life they had planned? *We've been lucky*, she thought. *We're both alive. I want to be grateful for the rest of my life. I want to live, conscious of the preciousness of it. I want to use every minute of this life that was given back to me.*

Normal life would return. She would force it to return for them—marriage, children, law school. She'd have to do it all at once. Five years they had lost; she was 26, almost 27. Somehow, she'd have to put all this behind her. She looked up at Barthold's face in the fading light and thought, *He doesn't know it yet, but that's how it's going to be.*

There was something important she had to do. It was her first day back home, and she was leaving on an errand. Her parents didn't understand; why couldn't it wait? Public transportation had not yet been restarted, so the choice was walking or bicycling. She found an old bicycle in the shed.

It took hours to get there. She could move only slowly, from time to time stopping to fight painful abdominal cramps.

For weeks now her innards were wreaking havoc, with short spells of peace between. It left her feeling weak. Exhausted when she arrived at the Van Waardens' house, she sat down on their step and found herself crying uncontrollably.

"Would you like to come in?" A middle-aged woman spoke to her. "I'll get you some water. Now, now, it'll be all right. You must've had bad news, you poor dear. These are awful times."

Marlise shook her head. Between violent sobs, she tried to explain, "I don't know what came over me. It's nothing. I just can't stop crying."

"I am Marian van Waarden. Please come in. This is my office. When you're ready, just come in that door."

There was a sink in the small office. Marlise splashed water on her face until she felt calmer and then knocked on the door. A group of people sat at a table.

"Am I interrupting?" she asked.

"Heavens, no! Please sit down. You must be tired," said Marian. "Have some strawberries with us, fresh from the garden."

It struck her that Marian had not introduced them. A young woman with light honey-colored hair and dark-brown eyes smiled at Marlise. She had a little boy on her lap.

At the other side of the table, she recognized Nettie van Vechtelen and her children. Nettie seemed distant, acknowledging Marlise's effusive greeting with a little nod. Nettie's daughter looked down at her plate, her thick dark hair hiding her face. Only the little boy slid off his chair, coming to her.

But Marian handed him a little basket. "Pieter, go out to the garden and pick us some more strawberries."

Marlise sat down. "Mrs. van Waarden, I have to know. I hope that you can tell me what happened to Riena. Where is she?"

Marian shook her head. "My dear, I think you better ask Henk. I really don't know what to tell you. But you know, her parents live across the road."

"Do you think I should ask them?"

Marian hesitated. "Perhaps later. I think you should talk to Henk first."

Marlise waited for him in the same small office, sitting in front of a desk. Shelves with bottles lined the walls.

He came in wearing his white coat, both hands outstretched. "How glad I am to see you," he said.

"Doctor van Waarden, I came to ask about Riena. We don't know what happened to her after her stay in the hospital."

He took his glasses off and put them in the pocket of his white coat. "My dear, nobody knows with certainty. She was taken away by the Germans. There are rumors..." He looked out the window and added, "Sometimes it's better not to know."

"Do you think I should go to her parents and ask them?"

He spun around. "I don't think so, no. They may resent you. They are suffering, the poor souls."

She insisted. "Is there any way to find out?"

He sat down again, locking eyes with her. "Her father was picked up when she was arrested. After she left the hospital, he was sent home with her clothes." There was a finality in his tone. "That is all they know. That is all we know."

44

"Look, Thea, the queen is walking outside," a voice said.

Thea went to the window. She saw Queen Wilhelmina strolling among the rose bushes in her private garden. The sight of that lonely gray-haired figure moved her. The queen had been such an isolated, plucky figure in London during all the war years, unwavering in her personal support of the resistance.

At first, the people had resented the queen's flight to London, but very quickly the wisdom of that decision had become apparent. She had sent her grandchildren and her daughter, the future queen, to safety in Ottawa, Canada. She herself remained active in London, a symbol of stubborn perseverance.

Now her palace in Apeldoorn had become a shelter for people returning from prisons and concentration camps. Many needed medical treatment; others simply had no place to go.

The newest arrivals were from Japanese camps in the former Dutch East Indies, where the war had lasted until August. Women with children now joined the released resistance fighters and lone Jewish survivors from prisons and German camps.

The two facing wings of the palace were designated for the shelter and makeshift hospital. The queen had retained the center portion of the building.

Carrying a tray, Thea walked through the long tunnel connecting the two wings. It really wasn't the most practical layout for its present use; it meant a lot of running back and forth through the tunnel for the staff.

"May I carry that for you?" a voice behind her asked.

Surprised, she recognized one of the few single men from the Japanese camps. He had not been seen talking to anybody. It was rumored that he had owned a tea plantation in Java.

"But of course," she replied.

Philip was propped up in bed, two young nurse's aides at his side. His sheer helplessness seemed to attract them. Thea sent them away.

"I have a man with me to help Philip up today."

She was grateful for the assistance. Philip was solid, heavy to handle. He had to be readied for the day's event, an invitation to tea from the queen. Thea gave him his painkillers. He was between operations; there were still bullets in his body. One was lodged near his spine.

His behavior was a cause for concern. He was passive and uncomplaining, and he spoke as little as possible. At night he did not sleep. Every time she checked on him, he just lay on his back as if thinking, his eyes wide open.

So it was startling to hear him ask the stranger, "Are you married?"

The man hesitated. "I am waiting for news about my wife and children. I haven't heard anything yet. We were separated—I mean, by the Japs. The men were interned in separate camps from the women and children."

Philip seemed to consider this. After a pause, he said, "I hope you will be together soon." He then turned to Thea. "Where are we going?"

"We are invited to tea by the queen. Now don't balk, Philip. There will be treats there." Food was still on coupons, a year after the liberation.

She handed him his crutches. His new helper from the Far East, Rob, stayed beside him.

They were late; most chairs were filled. Round tables were set up around the room. Sun streamed through the windows and large French doors.

Queen Wilhelmina moved from table to table. People were introduced to her by the coordinator of the shelter. She sat down here and there for a few minutes, dignified despite her dowdy appearance. At Thea's table, she joined long enough to talk to Philip about his upcoming operation. Then she turned to the planter from Java, saying, "We hope you will hear from your family. May God grant that they are safe."

Rob covered his eyes with his hand.

Through it all, Philip's attitude was one of benign indifference.

On Thursdays, Thea joined the physiotherapy session in the pool. She saw Philip, supported by the physiotherapist and Rob, stagger to the steps leading into the water. His bare chest showed many disfiguring scars. But once his body slid into the water, the metamorphosis took place. His still-powerful arms easily took over. It didn't matter that the movement of his legs seemed stiff and ineffectual. Rob swam beside him.

Thea and the physiotherapist remarked how beneficial this new friendship was between these two men. It also meant that the two women's full attention could be given to their other patient, a six-foot-five man who was completely bent over, his nose almost to his knees. He'd been forced by the Gestapo to spend eight months in a tiny cubicle of a cell and now was wrecked by arthritis.

When Philip was strong enough for his next operation, he asked to go home to Rotterdam for a weekend. Rob went with him on the train to deliver him to his relatives.

Thea saw them off.

On Monday, Philip had not yet returned as expected. Just then the news came that Rob's wife and 14-year-old daughter had been found. Although his infant twin sons had not survived the disease and hunger of camp life, he was overcome with joy and relief. He transformed before their eyes into a man with a purpose—his step was firmer, his eyes more direct, his voice louder.

The anticipation of this family reunion obscured the bad news when it came: on Tuesday, Philip's body was found in the river near his relatives' home.

Thea was packing Philip's few belongings when she came upon a slim wallet. With reluctance, she went through his papers. She studied a photograph of a young woman, a stranger. Puzzled, she fingered a piece of raw silk, the pale fragment cut irregularly.

A scrap of paper fell out, on which an English address was scribbled by a foreign hand.

Under it, printed and underlined, appeared the name Hugh.

On an impulse, she wrote a note to the English couple.

45

Free of fear at last.

But in its place had come a vague, nagging anxiety about his future in this new, complex world. At first, he had desperately looked for a job, anything to get out of the house, out from under the humiliating dependence on his parents. He wanted to live far away, married to Thea. He missed her. Any job would do, but there were few to be found in the struggling country.

"Connections, Steven!" his father urged. "You should at least have contacts from all those years in the Underground."

Steven despised them, the loudly clamoring groups of so-called resistance fighters. Where did they all suddenly spring up from? He refused to have anything to do with them.

"My connections are all dead." He saw the frustration in his father's face. Didn't his old man understand that he wanted to leave all that behind, to start fresh and forget the pain?

He had trouble sleeping. His mother found him sleepwalking, stalking through the house.

So it was back to university in the fall, along with reluctantly accepting his father's money. His classmates were three or four years younger, but he felt decades older. He resented the slow pace of his life and had trouble concentrating.

It didn't help to be compared to cousin Bert, who'd studied all through the war.

"He'll be finished next year," his mother said at the dinner table. "They're getting married when he graduates."

Steven put his fork and knife down and went to his room. He wiped his books off the table and dropped onto his bed.

He heard the bell ring and his mother calling.

"Steven! It's for you!" There was an urgency in her voice that made him run down three steps at a time.

The face in front of him was vaguely familiar, but the tense expectation in that fresh, round face jogged his memory: the photograph Hugo always kept beside his bed, from safe place to safe place.

He felt the blood drain from his face. His mind was blank, his lips frozen.

She took one look at him, then turned and ran away.

"You look as if you've seen a ghost." His mother looked concerned. "Who was it?"

"His fiancée, Hugo's," he stammered.

"For God's sake, why didn't you ask her in? Did she come all the way from Zeeland? Go after her! There's only one train south, and it leaves an hour from now."

He ran out of the door to the station. He had to find her. She didn't know, he thought frantically. How was it possible? It was months now since the liberation, and she didn't know?

At the station, he looked for her in the waiting room and on the platform. He was out of breath, desperate. *Where could she have gone?*

He went to bed early that night. His parents heard him tossing and turning in his sleep. They were still up when they saw him standing at the top of the stairs, his eyes staring, vacant.

"What is it, Steven?" his mother asked gently.

He pointed at the table in the dining room. "She is there." His arm remained outstretched in that direction. "She is sitting there, counting."

His father guided him back to his bed.

A few days later, his mother told him that his father was leaving on a business trip to Zeeland. Would he like to come along?

It was a clear fall day during the trip to Zeeland. The car, an old convertible, was drafty and noisy. Conversation with his father had become strained at best, so Steven did not mind that it was limited to the workings of the car and the route to take.

On entering the island of Walcheren, they fell silent. Dead trees lined the road, shriveled seaweed hanging from their branches. The once-green fields were covered with dark-brown mud.

In the villages the signs of battle were still evident, but nothing prepared them for the sight of the town of Vlissingen. His father, at the wheel, tried to find his way through streets where people were still clearing away rubble, a year after the fighting.

"You have the address?" his father asked.

"Not hers. Only the one of Hugo's parents."

"It'll be a miracle if it's still there and if they survived."

But it was there, one of the small red-roofed houses still standing in a narrow, curved street. Steven's hands were clammy with nervousness when he knocked on the front door.

A small man with a shock of gray hair invited them both in.

"You are very lucky people," Steven's father said, grabbing the man's hand.

Steven was aghast. The insensitivity!

"You are absolutely right," Hugo's father responded. "We were spared." His face was earnest—no need for polite small talk here.

"How is it in Middelburg?"

"Much better. Vlissingen was a strategically vital point for the Allies, at the entrance to the Scheldt."

The two older men had wandered into the front room, standing side by side at the window.

"You mean because of river access to Antwerp?" Steven's father asked.

"Right. After the disaster at Arnhem, the Allied forces had to give up on Rotterdam and Amsterdam, so they had to take Antwerp, the only port left."

"And the Germans were not going to let go of it."

"It was terrible. Thousands and thousands of young Canadians died in Zeeland. We're told over 10,000."

"So you believe the bombing of the dikes here was necessary?"

"We believe it helped end it, yes. It was an awful price to pay, though."

"Did a lot of people drown?" Steven asked, remembering the seaweed hanging high in the trees.

"We in our family were warned, thankfully, by the pamphlets the pilots dropped. Most people made it to higher ground like us, but all livestock drowned."

"What are the farmers going to do?" Steven wondered aloud.

"Well, first we have to find ways to get rid of the brine in the fields. Steven, will you ask my wife to bring us some coffee?"

Steven found her in the kitchen, wearing a flowered apron. She had Hugo's dark eyes and hair, the Zeelander's Celtic coloring, and a round face.

"I know Annie went to see you," she said as she filled a kettle at the tap. "When he didn't come home after the war was over in your part of the country, we knew, of course, that he was... dead. But she wouldn't give up. She thought he might be on his way, on foot, from somewhere in Germany."

She put cups and saucers on a tray and continued, "Every time somebody wandered in on foot she was more certain he'd come back. But I knew he'd try to contact us somehow. He was a good, good son." She wiped her eyes with the tip of her apron. "I have to admit, when we heard of someone finding his way back from Germany, I couldn't help but think... but they were usually men sent there to work, slave laborers."

"I am so sorry. I should have contacted you," Steven stammered. The kettle whistled, and the aroma of coffee filled the kitchen. "I'd like to see her, talk to her."

"I sent one of the kids to get her. Here she is now." She picked up the tray and left the kitchen.

The back door to the kitchen opened, and Annie stepped inside. He tried to remember the things he'd prepared in his head: Hugo did not suffer long. It was all very quick. I should have tried to find you, months ago.

Instead, he said, "He was my best friend." She cried against his shoulder. He continued, "I ran after you. I couldn't find you."

"I know, I saw you at the train station. I was hiding in the washroom. I couldn't face anyone."

"He kept your picture with him, always."

Somehow that calmed her. She straightened her shoulders and said, "Thank you. I can accept it now." She smiled pitifully at him. "No sense fooling myself any longer, is there?"

She opened the door. He tried to hold her back.

"No, I have to be alone now." She shut the door and disappeared into the ruins of the town.

In the front room, the two men were still talking. Hugo's father explained in detail the difficulties faced by the farmers of the island and the solutions to be found.

"We are a tough lot, and we know the sea and how to fight it. The trick is to get the salt out of the soil. The motto of Zeeland says it all: *Luctor et Emergo.* We struggle and surface." He poured *jenever* in small glasses.

Steven declined the gin. With his mission accomplished, he wanted to leave now.

On the way back his father was talkative, shouting over the roar of the motor, "He's a true schoolmaster, your friend's father. He knows a lot and likes to talk, doesn't he? They're a great lot, the Zeelanders." He looked out over the brown soggy fields. "They'll do it too. They'll turn it all around in half a dozen years."

That evening, Steven had a phone call from Thea. He wanted to tell her about his day and the relief he felt, but she had other things on her mind.

"Did you get the announcement?" she asked. "Marlise and Barthold are getting married."

An inexplicable anger rose in him. "How and why? They're both still in university. Where will they live? In that tiny room of his in Leiden? In her bedroom at her parents'?"

"Oh Steven, you sound like an old man. His parents offered to take them in. They had to take in a family anyway because of the housing shortage. They're keeping his room in Leiden for days they can't make it home."

"I'd never stay with my parents as a married man. It's bad enough to be dependent and single."

Her voice took on the patient quality he knew so well. "Of course it is, but we've waited long enough. My parents will take us in for the time being. I've been saving, not much, but with their help..."

He groaned. There was silence at the other end. Finally, he said, "Thea? Are you still there?"

"I'm still here, but not for much longer. I've had an invitation to go to England, so I'll take my savings and do just that."

The letter was left on her desk. This often happened when they did not want to be bothered. It meant: read it and file it.

"I'm nothing but a glorified secretary," Marlise muttered under her breath, "and paid less."

There were many handwritten pages. She turned them over without much interest. But then, on the last page, a familiar name: Alex van Vechtelen! She began to read, fascinated by the voice from the past.

How fast and how easily we forget, she thought. She searched through a filing cabinet, and somewhere stacked on the bottom she found a file folder filled with unanswered letters, marked "Van Vechtelen."

Folder under her arm, she challenged one of the junior partners. "Why did we never respond?"

"What did you dig up there? Oh, Van Vechtelen. He writes everybody all the time from prison. Good letters, they say, but I can't be bothered. He seems to think he deserves a new trial. Are you interested in that creep? Of all people, I didn't think you would be, Marlise."

"He was a friend of mine."

"Well, you were wrong. We still don't know how many deaths he's responsible for."

"Do you think I could take a look?"

"Not on our time; this firm will not be involved. Do as you please, but personally. Take it home." He turned away. He was Jewish and had lost his entire family in concentration camps; she knew it was unfair to expect him to empathize. In the daily struggle of performing tasks at work and at home, it was easy to forget that only a few years had gone by since they'd lived through the occupation - perhaps because most people were determined to try to keep it out of their minds. She put the file in her briefcase.

It hadn't been easy for her to finish law school as a married woman. In their one-room "apartment"—an attic room up three flights of stairs—she had had to cope with morning sickness before going to class. The relationship with her parents was strained; they resented Barthold and did not attend their simple wedding ceremony.

Holding the briefcase with one hand and steadying herself on a hanging strap with the other, she rode the crowded bus home. Home now meant cramped quarters on the top floor at her in laws'. Because of the housing crisis, many had been told to accept a second family in their house if it was deemed large enough by the authorities. What better solution for her in-laws than to invite their own son and his family to live with them?

At first she had resisted, impatient to be independent in a place of their own, but of course there was nothing to be found. After the baby was born even she had to admit to the benefits of the arrangement. The presence of her in-laws gave her the freedom to go to work.

Yet the reluctance lingered in a hidden resentment toward her mother-in-law. Often, when Marlise heard her daughter cry at night, she found the older woman already bent over the crib. It didn't help that the baby's room was a floor below their own quarters under the roof.

Barthold often came home late, after the baby had been bathed and put to bed. Curled up on the couch, Marlise was reading the Van

Vechtelen file when he came in. She showed him the letters and read from them.

"What do you think?" she asked.

"Go see him, by all means. That's what you want, isn't it?"

In the end, Marlise decided to go with Nettie. It would make the visit less formal, she told Barthold. After all, she was not representing the firm. She also knew it would make the visit more neutral; Alex and she shared memories no one else knew about.

Nettie, standing beside a small car, was waiting for Marlise outside the railroad station. In a beige suit and with a brown hat on short, straight-cut hair, Nettie waved the red scarf they had agreed would facilitate recognition.

Marlise climbed into the car and said, "I met you once at the Van Waardens'. Do you remember?"

"Of course." Nettie's gray, golden-flecked eyes returned a cool gaze to Marlise. A small but determined woman, Nettie maneuvered her car skillfully through the traffic. She explained it was a Citroën and very light: "I can push it out of the garage myself if need be." She looked sideways at Marlise. "Of course, that does not help in a collision—being so light, I mean."

"Mrs. van Vechtelen, do you still live in the same house?"

"Oh, no. I, er, *we* decided to sell it."

She changed gears before turning a corner. "I'm living in a small house in Noordwijk. The children go to school there."

A woman of few words, Nettie seemed strong and level-headed. *The type who'll stay with her man,* thought Marlise.

Alex had changed. There was much more gray at his temples, and he walked slightly bent over as if his shoulders sagged forward. Dark-rimmed glasses enlarged his blue eyes. Marlise felt a wave of pity wash over her.

"I've read your letters, the ones you sent to our office," she said.

The blue eyes registered surprise and gratitude. "Thank you for that, Marlise, and for coming."

"I don't know what you expect to be done. How much proof is there for what you're saying?"

"It's the truth, Marlise. I gave in at the end, the very end. But before that, I was absolutely loyal—careful, yes, but I never betrayed anybody or anything. When I was arrested, I was hoping that the time left before liberation was short. If only I could feed him little bits of information, then I could stall. Marlise, don't you understand? I tried to save my life…"

"All those years!" Nettie broke in. "All that time we risked our family, our home, our lives. Does that not carry any weight?"

"All that time," Marlise said, "and then something changed."

"It was fear—brute, naked fear. That is all," Alex said. His blue eyes seemed to protrude slightly behind his glasses, but they had not lost their directness.

There was a long stretch of silence. Then Marlise said softly, the words barely audible, "We were all afraid, all the time."

"Oh, what can I say? I guess I always thought I could pull it off." He looked forlorn.

Visiting time was over. Before leaving she promised, "I'll see what I can do."

"Marlise, thank you. You're the first ray of hope."

Back in the car, she regretted her words. "My firm will have nothing to do with it, and I am new there."

"So what can you do for him, then?" asked Nettie.

"I can be a witness. I can publicize his case. The problem is that it's his word only; there's no proof of coercion or anything."

Nettie seemed to consider this for some time. Finally, in a wavering voice, she said, "It means it may take years. Karin and Pieter…" She was unable to go on.

Marlise put her hand on Nettie's arm. "What will you do when he gets out?"

Nettie swerved to avoid a cyclist. "We will sell all our things. There is no life for us here. I have relatives in Australia; we'll just have to start again."

At the station she turned to Marlise, her voice steady now. "Thank you, Marlise. You're the only one who answered, the only one of all the Underground people we helped."

Marlise opened the car door. "There aren't many of us left."

47

"It's true, a plane crashed here in the fall of 1944: a British fighter plane, a Spitfire, I'm sure. The men inside? Not a chance. We couldn't be sure of how many, blown apart and burnt as they were. Papers? We looked for identity tags but didn't find anything. We buried them, whatever we found of them, in the old cemetery behind the church, in one grave. What else could we do? The minister will show you."

In the pale light of winter, Thea stood in the small cemetery. Bare branches cast shadows over gray stones sagging in moist black earth and sparse green grass. In a far corner was the pilots' grave, marked by a wooden cross.

"At the time, what could we do?" The minister sounded apologetic. "And even now, the British government doesn't seem too interested. Missing in action, you say? Well, chances are he didn't crash here at all. Most came down in the Zuiderzee—in Lake IJssel, I should say." He made a sweeping gesture toward the east. "Mark my words, they're going to uncover many wrecks on that sea bottom as they keep reclaiming land."

Thea's correspondence with Hugh's parents had led to this excursion, but she was unsure what to report back to them. They had seemed intensely anxious for some sort of closure. Now they wanted her to come to England, as if her visit would bring their son closer to them. Their last letter before her departure contained a troubling request. "They want me to bring some earth from that grave," she said to her friends. "Do they realize how much time it took to get there? That town is north of Amsterdam! I work here, in the middle of the country. I can't go back there before I leave."

"Why don't you bring some earth from here? How could they tell the difference?" one of her friends asked.

"Oh, no, I couldn't do that. That would be dishonest."

"Well, what if it's from the royal gardens?" another chimed in.

She laughed. It struck her as preposterous.

The crossing to England was rough. At first, she had enjoyed the newness of it—the meal on board, the insouciance of the crowd.

"The channel is choppy tonight, more than usual," someone at her table told her, lighting a cigarette. When the smoke reached her nostrils, she fled to the deck for fresh air.

A young woman leaned over the railing, retching, but turned a laughing face to her companion, who held her shoulders in support. He explained to Thea, "We're on our honeymoon."

Could they see her loneliness? What was she doing here?

In Harwich, she boarded a train to meet up with Hugh's older sister in London. The two began the long ride to England's North, facing each other.

"Do you have the earth from Hughie's grave?" Hugh's sister asked. "It means a lot to my Mum and Dad. They're not much for traveling —getting on in years, you know."

Thea remembered the corner of the small cemetery, the neglected communal grave. She shook her head. "Nobody is certain it's his grave."

"That doesn't matter; they're certain. It's the first certainty they've had, poor dears. My Mum was over 40 when she had Hughie. I already had my first job. Their only son, and he insisted on joining the air force, like Dad in the first war. They've never gotten over it and never will."

Thea took in the views of England that passed by—sloping fields separated by old stone walls, the tender green of early spring, the blossoming trees.

It was a row house in a small village. In the back, a garden stretched up a hill, with a gate at the end leading into fields beyond. Mum and Dad, frail for their years, fussed with a meal for their guest.

On the piano reposed a photograph of Hugh in uniform, a bouquet of fresh flowers beside it.

A dog licked her hands. "Hughie's dog. He recognizes you. He is happy you're here," Mum said.

In the morning, Dad woke Thea with a cup of steaming hot tea on a tray. "Hugh has told us that he is happy you're here," he said.

With a start she sat up, spilling the hot liquid on the tray.

"You see, he has a way of letting us know," Dad explained. "The flowers on the piano were moved during the night."

The large kitchen had an oven in the wall. Mum baked bread and pies by the light of the fire. The only outside light came through the door.

It was Hugh's birthday. Thea sat with Mum in front of a blazing fire, the older woman muttering to herself, waiting for her husband to come home from the pub, where he tried to drown his sorrow.

It was clear now she had made a mistake. She should have brought a small bowl of earth, and it would have taken on magical qualities for as long as they lived. Some day in the future—20, 50, or 100 years from now—his Spitfire might be found buried in mud, a watery grave for Hugh. Watching the couple cope with their grief was enlightening.

For Thea, cloaking reality in mystery had been beneath her, or perhaps beyond her scope. This whole country seemed to lend itself to it. The land's shapes were rounded, muted.

The return trip from Harwich to Hook of Holland was unremarkable. The sea was calm and the sky clear. When the ship approached the shore, Thea was struck by the sharp outline of the flat strip of land in the blue expanse of water and sky: home—sober and straightforward.

Before the gangplank was out, she saw a familiar tall figure on the quay. She waved frantically with both arms. She couldn't see anything else until they were holding each other, speechless.

Much later, Steven told her, "I quit school. I have a job. It's not much, but it's a beginning. It means moving away, but we'll find a small apartment for us."

Strange, it didn't seem that important anymore.

48

It couldn't have been a better day for the beach. The dunes stretch out on both sides of the road into the hazy blue distance. An endless procession of cyclists in light summer clothes moves along the bicycle path, hair blowing in the mild breeze.

Every now and then the path is obscured by the silver-green leaves of half-grown trees. Barthold is driving; beside him sits Steven, his young son on his lap. In the back, discussing feeding schedules, are the women, with Marlise and Barthold's little girl between them.

Marlise is holding her sleeping baby boy in her arms. With a deep sense of contentment, she looks out over the dune landscape, dotted with yellow and white flowering shrubs. Steven and Thea have come up for the weekend in their Citroën.

It has been fun to show them their growing family and their own house. Steven is good with the children; he has a quirky sense of humor that draws them out.

Marlise and Barthold lived with his parents during the difficult first years of their marriage. They were lucky because they could buy the house when his parents retired in the South of the country, where houses were available.

On one of the higher dunes to the right, she sees a flag on a tall pole. She taps Barthold on the shoulder. "I think we should," she says.

He looks over his shoulder in surprise. So far Marlise has avoided going to the cemetery in the dunes, even on the fourth of May, Remembrance Day. But she nods, so he swings the car around to go up the gravel path.

Barthold parks the car and takes his baby son from Marlise's arms. He walks in front, the baby looking over his shoulder, his red hair glinting a fiery gold in the sun.

In a little group, they trudge up the path. The sound of traffic has disappeared; all they hear is the hum of honeybees on the flowering trees and bushes. Marlise feels a tension mounting in her. Her throat feels dry.

Turning a corner, she sees the cemetery. A large rectangle has been dug out of the dune sand. To come close to the graves, they have to walk down a few steps. It is very still; even the insect sounds are hushed. She looks down at the grave markers, simple stones on slightly elevated ground, with inscriptions of dates of birth and death. Laid in double rows, the design allows them to walk on red brick paths between the graves. Nobody else is there. It's as if the world has disappeared.

Marlise has trouble breathing. She knows why. It's that she is fighting the reality of this recent past. What will happen if she faces it? She sits down on a stone step. "It's hot here. I'm dizzy."

Thea bends over her, but Barthold pulls her away. "Let her be alone for a few minutes." He places the baby in Marlise's lap.

Marlise sees Barthold trying to catch up with their daughter, who runs between the graves with the insouciance of a four-year-old, laughing at the efforts of her father. Steven and Thea are walking slowly, reading off names, row by row, their little boy between them.

Marlise hears other visitors coming up the path. She stands up and calls out to her daughter. A few paces beyond the cemetery is a bench, where she sits down with the little girl in the shade of a tree.

Soon the others join her, deep in conversation.

"Ask Marlise," Barthold said. "At her office, they hear from him regularly."

She looks up. "You mean Alex van Vechtelen? He writes us long letters, explaining that he deserves a new trial. He doesn't deny what he did but claims it was coercion, the only way to save his life."

Steven nods toward the graves. "They didn't talk or betray. As far as I'm concerned, Alex deserves the death penalty like the others. He was a traitor."

Marlise turns to him, her eyes darkening. "How can you judge him? You don't know if you, or any of us, would have acted any differently. People betrayed neighbors, and for what? Remember Hugo? We haven't heard of any investigation there, of course not. Right and wrong get muddled in wartime. As for me, I am going to do anything I can, with Nettie's help, to get a new trial for Alex."

Thea puts an arm around her shoulders. "Of course, Marlise, we will all help." She looks at Steven. He has become quiet at the mention of Hugo. It is a pain he will carry with him for the rest of his life.

"The death penalty does not belong in our country. I am glad they abolished it again," Marlise continues indignantly. "I believe him. I do feel sorry for him. He says that the good he did should in some measure offset what he did wrong."

Thea tries to interfere. "But Marlise, we don't know when he started to sell out. It's his word alone, after all."

Steven agrees. "God knows how many deaths he's responsible for! He deserves to be executed. He is at least responsible for Tony's death, that is certain."

Thea puts her arm around him. "Oh Steven, you are always so extreme. Everything is black or white for you."

Barthold sits down beside Marlise. The baby pulls himself up to stand on his father's knees and tugs at his hair.

"Thea, I hear that you know what happened to Philip in the end," Barthold says. "I never particularly liked him, but he didn't give in. He didn't talk."

"I saw him in Apeldoorn," Thea says. "He'd had many operations and needed even more. He still had bullets in his body. You should have seen his chest! The scars were awful, especially the ones from the bayonets of his interrogators. He had trouble walking, but there were always people willing to help. They loved him. He never complained. More than one nurse gladly would have spent the rest of her life with him."

She looks at Steven, who has hoisted their son on his shoulders, ready to leave. She continues, "And then, when we sent him off on his first weekend back home in Rotterdam, it happened. They found him in the river. He drowned."

"He didn't drown." Steven shakes his head. "That wasn't an accident."

Barthold stands up. "You may be right. He had shady commie friends. The party, you know. They are sinister."

"On the other hand, he had a lot of pain. At the hospital, they thought that he did not want to live his life as a physical wreck." But Thea sounds doubtful. "Fact is, he still was a good swimmer."

Quietly, they go back down the path.

Marlise voices a thought that has lain dormant at the back of her mind: "Was Riena ever found?"

"Who knows?" Steven says. He stands still, looking south over the dunes, his arms wrapped around the little boy's legs. "This is not the only resistance cemetery. Besides, some families wanted to make their own arrangements."

Barthold hands the baby to Marlise; his daughter wants a piggyback ride. Hoisting her on his back, he says, "Those two, Philip and Riena—there was something going on." Barthold parks behind the last row of dunes. In the parking lot are several German cars; the Dutch coast has become a favored holiday destination for West Germans.

Marlise grabs a bundle of towels and runs after her daughter on the sandy path, up the last dune. From her childhood memory comes the familiar rush of excitement and anticipation.

There it is. Reaching the top she catches her breath; it is so beautiful, always changing, always impressive. Today the wide expanse of water is a deep slate blue fringed by white surf. It is just past ebb's lowest point. The beach is wide, and the waves surge forward.

The golden sand is dotted with colorful parasols and flags. The dunes rise behind, with rough, long grass waving in the shifting sand. Along the fringe of the dunes, at regular intervals, stand the concrete bunkers built by the Germans, a permanent reminder of their readiness for an invasion from the North Sea, an invasion that never came.

They settle down next to a beach entrance, to allow for a quick exit when the children get tired.

Beside them, people have dug a large pit, walled like a fortress. Chairs and a windscreen have been set up inside its walls.

Marlise notices Steven's gaze. "They're German tourists," she explains, pointing out several other similar forts. "They claim it for their own during their stay."

"An invasion of sorts after all, huh?" Steven says with a wry smile. Behind them, some children play in and around the bunkers.

They stretch out in the soft, still-cool sand. The baby sits on a towel under an umbrella, trying out two brand-new teeth on a biscuit. The two- and four-year-old are busy filling pails with sand.

"We've had incredible luck," Steven says. "Think about it. Of all the guys I started with in the beginning, only two survived—you and I."

"And Marlise." Barthold strokes her shoulder. "She was also there from the beginning."

Marlise, lying on her stomach, pours a fistful of fine sand. "And Alex." She resents their silence and sits up. "Why not mention him? He was with us until almost the end. Can you tell me why we are so hard on our own? Those Georgians we saw here in German uniform —remember them? Now we know they joined the German army to save their skins. We think of them as heroes, for God's sake."

"Because they revolted." Thea has followed their story.

"But that was in April, a few weeks before the end of the war!" Marlise feels her anger rise.

"Because they were slaughtered, then, fighting the Germans with their own weapons." Steven is getting impatient.

"There were a couple hundred survivors because the islanders hid them, and they went back home. We don't remember, do we, that in the battle a hundred Dutch people were killed, too, on the island."

Marlise digs her heels in the cool sand. "I think we should help Alex. What about all the people who did nothing, never did anything? What he did before should count for something. After all, he delivered *Kommandant* Gunther Blechmann to us."

There is no reply. They are quiet, thoughtful.

Finally, Steven turns to her. "That's true. The *Kommandant* probably would be living in South America by now if he hadn't."

Barthold agrees. "The truth is that right and wrong were not as clear-cut then, for all of us. But still, there was a line drawn somewhere, and Alex crossed it."

Marlise feels she is winning. "I for one will come forward if he gets his time in court."

Barthold laughs. "This is not a courtroom. It's a beach." He puts his hand on her arm. "Why don't you go teach your daughter how to stay on her feet in the surf?"

Marlise runs toward the water, her little girl skipping ahead of her. Just having shed her baby fat, she looks like Barthold, lanky already, but his faded blond is of an almost silvery hue, so light, in her.

It is still early summer; the cold of the water takes her breath away. Standing sideways against the force of the waves, she holds her daughter by both hands in the strong surf. When a cresting wave approaches, she lifts her high. The little girl squeals with delight. The intense happiness! For the moment it's all there is.

Afterward, they exuberantly sprinkle the men and Thea with the icy seawater and laugh at their gasps and screams.

A ball rolls from the sand fort beside them. A little girl comes sliding after it. Marlise sees her daughter run to the ball to retrieve it.

The two girls are standing in the sunlight, smiling at each other. Instinctively, Marlise jumps up, but Barthold holds her back.

"Let them play. They have to start over."

She watches her daughter climb the side of the fortress. German voices and music rise from the pit.

"I wonder if our children will ever know what happened here?" Thea says.

Steven looks up at the two little girls, sitting side by side in the sand. "They'll know, but will they understand?"

"I hope they won't." Marlise speaks with passion. "I hope they will never understand."

Sitting down again, Marlise rests her elbows on her knees. Her chin cupped in her hands, she stares at the sea. Children are playing along the edge. So many ships, so many lives lost, yet nothing in the blue surface betrays their tragedies.

The waves roll in, spraying foam. Their eternal sound drowns out the human voices.

AFTERWORD

In this historical fiction story, which I wrote about 30 years ago, I attempted to document life in the western part of the Netherlands during the last year of the German occupation in World War II. When war was declared in September 1939, I was 14 years old. The German army invaded the Netherlands on May 10, 1940. When the war in Europe finally ended on May 4, 1945, it was on my 20th birthday. The Germans were still in town; we were waiting for Allied forces to arrive.

I tried to limit myself to experiences I had and things I saw or heard firsthand during that time, the last year of occupation, 1944–45. The Netherlands and Norway were, for some reason, the two countries burdened with a civilian German administration from the beginning of the occupation. In the Netherlands under Seyss-Inquart (I may misspell his name but will never forget), one of the first decisions the German occupying forces had imposed was to cut off all outside information. Newspapers were shut down or taken over; radios were confiscated. In the first chapter I describe how in our home we hid the small radio, which we ("illegally") had kept, in the foot of a table.

Rumors were shared by word of mouth; there is no way of verifying which ones were true. During the war, the rumor came to us that a lawyer in The Hague had built a relationship with the German *Ortskommandant* by playing chess with him, was able to gain access to the notorious prison in Scheveningen where resistance fighters and other political prisoners were held, and perhaps even had been able to get reprieve for some of them.

I used my imagination to build a story line on the relationship between these two individuals, Alex the lawyer and Gunther the *Kommandant*. Both are entirely fictional. The fact that I worked in a lawyers' office in The Hague between 1946 and 1948 helped me with location and setting.

The characters in the story are fictional, but what they experienced were real events. For example, the character of Anton, later Tony, was based on what happened to so-called Engelandvaarders I have known. He was one of the agents dropped by the British behind the lines in the infamous *Englandspiel*. Like the two I mentioned earlier, he was immediately detained by the Germans and imprisoned in Scheveningen, from where he escaped using the unarmed combat skills he had learned.

On the other hand, Steven is solely based on my brother. When he plays a part, I let him speak for himself, as I remember what I saw or what he shared with me during the war and afterward. Also, he relived his experiences and recounted them to me when we walked in The Hague in 2006. Hugo is based on his friend Nico, whom he saw arrested by the Gestapo and who was executed within 24 hours.

Women as couriers, such as Marlise and Riena, were essential in the later years of the war. At that time, men between the ages of 18 and 45 were rounded up for forced labor in German factories. When no one showed up voluntarily, raids were launched by the military to capture all men and boys they could find. Women and girls took on the job of courier for the resistance, generally called the Underground. For Marlise and Riena I used my own, though limited, experiences as a courier during the last year of the war and, in Marlise's case, also during the aftermath, when life returned to closer to normal.

For Riena's story, I used my own experience of being "recruited" as a courier by a friendly neighbor, a doctor. In several chapters I describe these courier "errands" exactly as they occurred.

Marlise is loosely based on a rumor we heard at the time about a redheaded girl who received roses in her prison cell. All references to her personally are my imagination.

Some of the methods of torture and their long-term aftereffects I saw in a few patients when I worked in Het Loo Palace, such as in the stories of Riena and Philip. The manner of Riena's tragic death is based on the report we received at the time of my cousin, a university student in Utrecht. She had been arrested transporting a German military uniform.

Beyond that, as well as incorporating my actual courier experiences in the resistance, Riena's story and relationships are fictional; I knew almost nothing about my cousin's life. What we heard is that she was transporting an SS uniform in a suitcase by bicycle when she was arrested. We were told she was shot and killed somehow during transportation between the prison and the hospital. Her father, my uncle, who was also detained, received her clothes in a paper bag upon his release. He knew then that his daughter had died. I met my uncle several times in the following years, but his daughter's fate was never mentioned. Some subjects must be avoided. For this novel, I used one possible scenario that reached us as a rumor at the time. To me, it explains the silence afterward.

I thank the readers of this manuscript in Canada, the US, and the Netherlands, and in particular my sister-in-law, who remembered it all. I owe a debt of gratitude to my son Allan for hours of work editing.

I thank my son Tom, who found the 30-year-old manuscript and who has been the driving force behind bringing it to this point.

In 1942, as a 16-year-old high schooler, I chose for my presentation in a Dutch literary class a poem by Hendrik Marsman, Dies Irae [Day of Wrath], published posthumously in 1941. He drowned in an explosion on June 21, 1940, while trying to escape to Great Britain as a passenger on the SS *Berenice*. Dutch sources claim there was an explosion in the engine room; German sources claim the ship was torpedoed by a U-boat. The only passenger to survive was Hendrik's widow. I remember some of the phrases of this poem, truly a premonition. Here is my inept translation:

> Forced down under low morals
>   of a somber, godforsaken time,
>   we move warily among the beasts
>   to whom we slowly are prepared as prey. ...
>   Oh the fury, helpless to the teeth,
>   to be exposed to this grey purgatory.
>   When will this Babel then burn down
>   from its foundations to the dark skies?
>   When will the horizon light again
>   with the faint dawn glimmer of our Hope?
>   She doesn't need grand vistas
>   to lift herself from death...

Extracts of "Dies Irae", *Collected Poems* (1941), H. Marsman

NOTES

The following is a list of actual events experienced by the author that have appeared in the story.

THE RADIO. In our home, we hid a small radio in exactly this way. All radios were confiscated by the German authorities.

DOUBLE FLOOR IN CLOSET. In our parental home, the hiding place was underneath the clothes closet, not behind the back wall. Apparently these hiding places became too well known to German searchers.

PASSWORD. A password often used was "Scheveningen," the name of the coastal town bordering The Hague, because Germans could not pronounce the Dutch sound "sch."

ILLEGAL. A term used to refer to resistance fighters (or resistance workers).

ANNOYING BRITISH FLIER. British fliers were thought to be more difficult to control in risky situations than American fliers.

DANGER OF SMOKE. Smoke rising from a wood fire was another reported incident.

BOMBARDMENT OF NIJMEGEN. The accidental killing of Dutch citizens by Allied forces was collateral damage.

MENSUR SCAR. Many high-ranking officers had this badge of honor on their cheeks from fencing in university days.

Execution of hostages. This occurred in a public place in several cities to retaliate against acts of sabotage and resistance. The replacement of hostages with political prisoners did indeed happen.

An old windmill. A mill was still used in secret to grind wheat into flour in the place where our family lived.

Arrest of a young father. I learned about this in my community through meeting his wife in a manner similar to that recounted in this chapter.

Engelandvaarders. Anton and Leo became so-called Engelandvaarders: resistance fighters who escaped to England in small boats, in this case based on the story of two men in our neighborhood. When they returned to the continent, Germans were waiting for them; see *Das Englandspiel*. One escaped and survived.

Underground printing press. I saw one of these presses in Haarlem; this is a description of that location.

Bicycle tires. Tires were patched so many times that people resorted to wooden rims, which were not any more comfortable!

Donations stolen and sent to Germany. My family had in fact made this very mistake in the first year of the German occupation by donating a gift of furniture accompanied by a letter.

A baby girl. A baby spent a few months in my family's home.

On Christians and atheists. This pronouncement was often heard during World War II.

Identity check. The Germans often used this method to check identity cards on trains and in train stations.

Questioning of the Resistance. It was not uncommon.

Precise bombing. The precise bombing of a particular registry office, with the buildings on both sides left unscathed, obviously was an inside job. As I recall, most employees were supposed to have left the building. The death of Dutch civilians ("collateral damage") occurred often when Allied bombers hit targets on Dutch soil.

The red-haired prisoner. There was a rumor of a redheaded prisoner in The Hague and a commander who brought her flowers in her cell.

Student protest in 1941. Dutch university students protested against the firing of Jewish professors. In retaliation, the Nazi

German occupiers closed all universities in the Netherlands from then on, until the end of the war.

FORCED EMIGRATION. Under this scheme "Germanic" Dutch people would have been forced to emigrate to "Slavic" Poland, one of the bizarre ideas of Hitler and his regime.

BOMBARDMENT OF ROTTERDAM'S CITY CENTER. The bombing by the invading Germans in May 1940, originally a threat to force the Netherlands' surrender, was nonetheless executed despite that surrender. It destroyed Rotterdam's entire old centrum.

HENK AND MARIAN VAN WAARDEN. He a family physician and she a pharmacist, Henk and Marian van Waarden are based on a couple who was close to our family and neighbors.

RECRUITMENT INTERVIEW. This describes exactly my recruitment interview, involving English cigarettes and an Austrian in the Totenkopf Regiment, although it was conducted by Dr. van D., a Belgian doctor, also a neighbor and a brave young father of small children.

NATURAL RAW SILK. The silk from recovered Allied parachutes was used for dresses and skirts. I have never been lucky enough to own one, but I remember seeing and holding the material.

SORES AND INFECTIONS. Most patients asking for help were suffering from infections and sores due to the lack of soap and even the most rudimentary disinfectants and bandages.

RISKY PLAN. This risky plan was carried out and pulled off as described, except for the part of the tank trap in the dunes, something I saw much later.

DAS ENGLANDSPIEL. The unbelievable errors (or was it something else, something more sinister?) of the British intelligence cost many agents their lives.

HARBOR OF IJMUIDEN. In 1940, when the Dutch realized that the British would do no more than sink ships in the harbor of IJmuiden and withdraw southward, citizens were shocked—until they realized that soon Belgium and France would also be overrun by the German blitzkrieg.

AUSWEIS. An *Ausweis*, or permit, was necessary to ride a bicycle. I had a permit for the bicycle I used, on the pretense that I needed it to get to work as a telephone operator for the German army. It is also true, as I later found out, that the bicycle did not have the same number as the permit.

Little boy in a high chair. This is a memory of a house in The Hague, where shooting practice was going on in the basement. The mother's name was Jo.

Loudspeakers. Loudspeakers were indeed everywhere. Hitler's menacing voice, with falling and rising crescendos, was inescapable on the day after the assassination attempt.

Singing. Troops sang the song "Erika" as I passed them on one of my errands; their threatening presence seemed ironically juxtaposed with the little flower mentioned in the song.

The "arrest" of the baby. Although I based the character of Ada on one of my childless aunts, the baby was in fact taken from an incredibly brave woman in our area, where one of the two Engelandvaarders, a young Jewish man, had also been hiding. In a rage, she gave the men who took the child a piece of her mind to the point that they did not arrest her. Not long before, the baby had been in our house for a few weeks.

Westerbork. This child and her brother did indeed wind up in Westerbork, a "transit camp." We were told that they were protected by a woman, a stranger. The baby girl and her brother survived and moved to the United States to live with family.

Baby carriage. The mother of the child (Greta in the story), did indeed make several trips to the apartment with the baby carriage to retrieve the weapons left there after their friend's arrest and execution. Her husband was of an age that he could be arrested at any time for work in Germany. I visited the couple as described.

Noordeinde Palace. This again is a fact: my brother Evert (Steven in the story) spent some time hiding in one of the bedrooms of the royal palace in The Hague, guarded unwittingly by Germans on the street in front of the palace. One of his friends was with him. During our walk of reminiscence, he pointed out the spot on the second floor on the right.

liberation of Brussels. Brussels was liberated on September 3, 1944. At this point, the liberation of western Holland, with the cities of

Amsterdam, Rotterdam, and The Hague, seemed no more than days away.

BREDA. On September 5, 1944, the advance of the Allied armies into Breda created a day of such confusion that the Dutch named it Dolle Dinsdag (Mad Tuesday). The German army seemed to be fleeing, and the suppressed population burst out in celebration, not knowing that the worst was still to come.

GERMAN SEARCHERS. Germany SS, Gestapo, and other searchers no doubt had been aware of hiding places in closets and were prepared to shoot first.

MIDDELBURG. The capital of the province of Zeeland, Middelburg, situated in the center of the island, and its harbor city Vlissingen in the South, also saw severe fighting and extensive damage.

A SHORT FLICKER OF HOPE. The progress that seemed to be made but was stopped at Arnhem—with tragic losses on the British side—was recounted in the film *A Bridge Too Far*.

RAILROAD STRIKE. London called a railroad strike to aid the Allied invasion.

STATIONED GERMAN SOLDIERS. Surrounded by Allied front lines, 100,000 German soldiers remained stationed in the occupied Northwest of the Netherlands.

KILLING OF A GERMAN OFFICER. A high-ranking German officer was killed near the village of Putten, and the German retaliation was merciless.

COURIER ERRAND. This chapter describes, detail by detail, the experience of one particular errand I did for the resistance. For some reason, I also remember clearly that I seemed to know the voice of the man who handed me the blueprints, but I was unable to recognize who it was. He did indeed wear the silly disguise of a sort of Groucho Marx mustache and dark-rimmed spectacles.

MACHINE GUNS. On this trip, I saw such machine guns set up on street corners. The streets were deserted.

MAUER-MUUR. It is true that we called the concrete structure blocking off major roads going into (or out of) the city the *Mauer-muur*. There was a narrow passage in the center of the concrete wall.

PERSONSBEWEIS. Every citizen had to carry a *Personsbeweis*, the

German word for "identity card." As a teenager I had one, but I do not know if children under 12 had to carry one on them. Besides a photograph, it also had a fingerprint.

FAREWELL PARTY. I attended a farewell party of a Jewish family before they went underground. Their teenage children attended the same high school as I did.

CLOTHING AND HOUSEHOLD ITEMS. The description of clothing and household items is adapted from a memory from 1945, just after the war, when a middle-aged woman was on duty with me as a helper to allow concentration camp survivors to reclaim such items. Very few showed up. One tough customer showed me the hole in his head where German guards had tried to kill him.

CHILDREN TO AUSCHWITZ. We were indeed told that the two children were on a transport to Auschwitz on September 4.

ROUNDING UP IN ROTTERDAM. As far as I know, these numbers are accurate for the raid in Rotterdam that rounded up men for forced labor in factories in Germany.

SECRET SUPPLIES. In the days following May 4, 1945, officers of the Canadian Hastings and Prince Edward Regiment told us about these underground supplies of food, fuel, and arms; I have never since heard anything more about this.

RAID AND ARREST. This chapter is almost word for word the experience of my brother Evert (Steven in the story) and his friend when they were arrested during a raid in The Hague, a raid by German military to round up all men they could find for forced labor in Germany.

ESCAPE. This chapter describes my brother and his friend's escape from German custody while they were waiting for transport to Germany in a border province in the northeastern Netherlands. The rest of the chapter describes the conditions in the western provinces of North and South Holland as well as the German offensive in the Ardennes in December 1944.

V-1 (UNMANNED ROCKET). I first heard and saw a V-1 as I stood in line waiting.

COAL. This is based on a memory of a soldier aiming at a civilian scooping up some coal.

Porridge. This chapter describes an experience I had eating porridge during the winter months of 1945.

Relay of couriers. The relay of couriers in Utrecht refers to the experiences of my cousin, an Utrecht University student, and the way she died, as far as is known.

Search for food. This chapter was inspired by a trek for food my father and I made sometime in February 1945. The idea of a lawyer–client relationship between my father and the farmer is fictional. We stopped at a random farm and bought 30 pounds of unmilled grain for ƒ3,000 and a pair of boots.

Hongerlopers (hunger walkers). Along the highway went an endless stream of people in search of food.

Food program. This chapter describes the experience my older sister Sophie and I had of weighing and measuring children in a doctor's office. The children in the worst state of starvation were selected for a limited food program, set up by physicians in the area.

Tulip bulbs. People ate tulip bulbs; I remember doing so myself.

Food drop. The one-time food drop from the Swedish Red Cross included one loaf of bread and one package of margarine per person.

Explosions; order from London. In reality, this happened at Santpoort station, behind our house.

Bombing of Bezuidenhout. The bombardment of the Bezuidenhout neighborhood in The Hague was said to be a navigational error by the RAF; it most likely had been meant for Benoordenhout, thought to be the area of a V-2 launching pad.

Attack on German vehicles. The vehicles turned out to be the convoy of a highly placed official, Hanns Albin Rauter, and therefore the attack had terrible consequences.

Eardrum perforation. Germans perforated eardrums as torture. It had happened during an interrogation to a person who later was one of my patients at Het Loo Palace.

Georgians. Men from the Georgian SSR were rounded up and moved to the island of Texel, just north of the province of North Holland; almost all were killed there.

Bayonets. A young patient in Het Loo Palace was terribly scarred by bayonets; he underwent multiple operations. He experienced the ordeal after trying to escape from an ambush by swimming across a canal.

Food drops. Food drops were certainly unforgettable for anyone who witnessed one, but they were strictly controlled by German troops.

Requisitioned bicycles. Bicycles—in fact, anything on wheels—were frequently requisitioned by the Germans. This happened to my aunt in front of our house. On my birthday, May 4, 1945, she appeared on a well-maintained bicycle, kept hidden for years (with the original tires!), to celebrate the end of the war together with our family. Two armed Germans rode away on her bicycle, one on the rear bike rack, shouldering his rifle. We locked eyes as I watched them disappear.

Shooting rampage. According to eyewitness reports of May 7, 1945, a shooting rampage by Germans took place on the Dam in Amsterdam.

Mass graves. The mass graves in the dunes are now located in a cemetery near Bloemendaal, just off a major road connecting Haarlem to a popular beach.

Plane crash. With help from my father, who drove a car, and local cemetery caretakers, I was able to locate the graves of three British fliers; one of them was thought to be the son of a couple with whom I had corresponded. At the time, townspeople had buried them in a small cemetery located in one of the villages on the then Zuiderzee, now Lake IJssel, halfway between Amsterdam and the north end of the province of North Holland.

German bunkers. At the time of writing this, these bunkers certainly appeared to be permanent—built as solid as German thoroughness could. At present, I believe attempts have been made to destroy them in some locations.

ABOUT THE AUTHOR

Johanna Kinney was born in 1925 in Java, Indonesia, in what was then a Dutch colony. In 1930 her family returned to live in the Netherlands. During wartime both she and her brother Evert were involved in the Underground, her brother subsequently knighted for distinguished service and bravery. Her own lived experience and those of her associates during wartime inspired *Dutch Defense.*

After the war, Johanna married and had two children in Belgium. Her Dutch husband died; she eventually remarried, this time wedding a Canadian officer she'd met 15 years earlier during the time of liberation. Though widowed a second time only 15 years later, she remained persistent: returning to a full-time career at age 50; providing for her five sons while earning degrees in psychology and education; becoming an accomplished educator; and ultimately designing a program for, and instructing, gifted students. She remained an educator into her late 60s.

After retiring in 1993, she wrote the first complete version of this book, both at her house in Montreal and largely while she was caring for a new grandchild in Boston. Today she lives in Ottawa, Canada.

AMSTERDAM PUBLISHERS
HOLOCAUST LIBRARY

The series **Holocaust Survivor Memoirs World War II** consists of the following autobiographies of survivors:

Outcry. Holocaust Memoirs, by Manny Steinberg

Hank Brodt Holocaust Memoirs. A Candle and a Promise, by Deborah Donnelly

The Dead Years. Holocaust Memoirs, by Joseph Schupack

Rescued from the Ashes. The Diary of Leokadia Schmidt, Survivor of the Warsaw Ghetto, by Leokadia Schmidt

My Lvov. Holocaust Memoir of a twelve-year-old Girl, by Janina Hescheles

Remembering Ravensbrück. From Holocaust to Healing, by Natalie Hess

Wolf. A Story of Hate, by Zeev Scheinwald with Ella Scheinwald

Save my Children. An Astonishing Tale of Survival and its Unlikely Hero, by Leon Kleiner with Edwin Stepp

Holocaust Memoirs of a Bergen-Belsen Survivor & Classmate of Anne Frank, by Nanette Blitz Konig

Defiant German - Defiant Jew. A Holocaust Memoir from inside the Third Reich, by Walter Leopold with Les Leopold

In a Land of Forest and Darkness. The Holocaust Story of two Jewish Partisans, by Sara Lustigman Omelinski

Holocaust Memories. Annihilation and Survival in Slovakia, by Paul Davidovits

From Auschwitz with Love. The Inspiring Memoir of Two Sisters' Survival, Devotion and Triumph Told by Manci Grunberger Beran & Ruth Grunberger Mermelstein, by Daniel Seymour

Remetz. Resistance Fighter and Survivor of the Warsaw Ghetto, by Jan Yohay Remetz

My March Through Hell. A Young Girl's Terrifying Journey to Survival, by Halina Kleiner with Edwin Stepp

Roman's Journey, by Roman Halter

Memoirs by Elmar Rivosh, Sculptor (1906-1967). Riga Ghetto and Beyond, by Elmar Rivosh

The series **Holocaust Survivor True Stories WWII** consists of the following biographies:

Among the Reeds. The true story of how a family survived the Holocaust, by Tammy Bottner

A Holocaust Memoir of Love & Resilience. Mama's Survival from Lithuania to America, by Ettie Zilber

Living among the Dead. My Grandmother's Holocaust Survival Story of Love and Strength, by Adena Bernstein Astrowsky

Heart Songs. A Holocaust Memoir, by Barbara Gilford

Shoes of the Shoah. The Tomorrow of Yesterday, by Dorothy Pierce

Hidden in Berlin. A Holocaust Memoir, by Evelyn Joseph Grossman

Separated Together. The Incredible True WWII Story of Soulmates Stranded an Ocean Apart, by Kenneth P. Price, Ph.D.

The Man Across the River. The incredible story of one man's will to survive the Holocaust, by Zvi Wiesenfeld

If Anyone Calls, Tell Them I Died. A Memoir, by Emanuel (Manu) Rosen

The House on Thrömerstrasse. A Story of Rebirth and Renewal in the Wake of the Holocaust, by Ron Vincent

Dancing with my Father. His hidden past. Her quest for truth. How Nazi Vienna shaped a family's identity, by Jo Sorochinsky

The Story Keeper. Weaving the Threads of Time and Memory - A Memoir, by Fred Feldman

Krisia's Silence. The Girl who was not on Schindler's List, by Ronny Hein

Defying Death on the Danube. A Holocaust Survival Story, by Debbie J. Callahan with Henry Stern

A Doorway to Heroism. A decorated German-Jewish Soldier who became an American Hero, by Rabbi W. Jack Romberg

The Shoemaker's Son. The Life of a Holocaust Resister, by Laura Beth Bakst

The Redhead of Auschwitz. A True Story, by Nechama Birnbaum

Land of Many Bridges. My Father's Story, by Bela Ruth Samuel Tenenholtz

Creating Beauty from the Abyss. The Amazing Story of Sam Herciger, Auschwitz Survivor and Artist, by Lesley Ann Richardson

On Sunny Days We Sang. A Holocaust Story of Survival and Resilience, by Jeannette Grunhaus de Gelman

Painful Joy. A Holocaust Family Memoir, by Max J. Friedman

I Give You My Heart. A True Story of Courage and Survival, by Wendy Holden

In the Time of Madmen, by Mark A. Prelas

Monsters and Miracles. Horror, Heroes and the Holocaust, by Ira Wesley Kitmacher

Flower of Vlora. Growing up Jewish in Communist Albania, by Anna Kohen

Aftermath: Coming of Age on Three Continents. A Memoir, by Annette Libeskind Berkovits

Not a real Enemy. The True Story of a Hungarian Jewish Man's Fight for Freedom, by Robert Wolf

Zaidy's War. Four Armies, Three Continents, Two Brothers. One Man's Impossible Story of Endurance, by Martin Bodek

The Glassmaker's Son. Looking for the World my Father left behind in Nazi Germany, by Peter Kupfer

The Apprentice of Buchenwald. The True Story of the Teenage Boy Who Sabotaged Hitler's War Machine, by Oren Schneider

Good for a Single Journey, by Helen Joyce

Burying the Ghosts. She escaped Nazi Germany only to have her life torn apart by the woman she saved from the camps: her mother, by Sonia Case

American Wolf. From Nazi Refugee to American Spy. A True Story, by Audrey Birnbaum

Bipolar Refugee. A Saga of Survival and Resilience, by Peter Wiesner

The series **Jewish Children in the Holocaust** consists of the following autobiographies of Jewish children hidden during WWII in the Netherlands:

Searching for Home. The Impact of WWII on a Hidden Child, by Joseph Gosler

See You Tonight and Promise to be a Good Boy! War memories, by Salo Muller

Sounds from Silence. Reflections of a Child Holocaust Survivor, Psychiatrist and Teacher, by Robert Krell

Sabine's Odyssey. A Hidden Child and her Dutch Rescuers, by Agnes Schipper

The Journey of a Hidden Child, by Harry Pila and Robin Black

The series **New Jewish Fiction** consists of the following novels, written by Jewish authors. All novels are set in the time during or after the Holocaust.

The Corset Maker. A Novel, by Annette Libeskind Berkovits

Escaping the Whale. The Holocaust is over. But is it ever over for the next generation? by Ruth Rotkowitz

When the Music Stopped. Willy Rosen's Holocaust, by Casey Hayes

Hands of Gold. One Man's Quest to Find the Silver Lining in Misfortune, by Roni Robbins

The Girl Who Counted Numbers. A Novel, by Roslyn Bernstein

There was a garden in Nuremberg. A Novel, by Navina Michal Clemerson

The Butterfly and the Axe, by Omer Bartov

To Live Another Day. A Novel, Elizabeth Rosenberg

A Worthy Life. Based on a True Story, by Dahlia Moore

The series **Holocaust Heritage** consists of the following memoirs by 2G:

The Cello Still Sings. A Generational Story of the Holocaust and of the Transformative Power of Music, by Janet Horvath

The Fire and the Bonfire. A Journey into Memory, by Ardyn Halter

The Silk Factory: Finding Threads of My Family's True Holocaust Story, by Michael Hickins

~

The series **Holocaust Books for Young Adults** consists of the following novels, based on true stories:

The Boy behind the Door. How Salomon Kool Escaped the Nazis. Inspired by a True Story, by David Tabatsky

Running for Shelter. A True Story, by Suzette Sheft

The Precious Few. An Inspirational Saga of Courage based on True Stories, by David Twain with Art Twain

~

The series **WW2 Historical Fiction** consists of the following novels, some of which are based on true stories:

Mendelevski's Box. A Heartwarming and Heartbreaking Jewish Survivor's Story, by Roger Swindells

A Quiet Genocide. The Untold Holocaust of Disabled Children WW2 Germany, by Glenn Bryant

The Knife-Edge Path, by Patrick T. Leahy

Brave Face. The Inspiring WWII Memoir of a Dutch/German Child, by I. Caroline Crocker and Meta A. Evenbly

When We Had Wings. The Gripping Story of an Orphan in Janusz Korczak's Orphanage. A Historical Novel, by Tami Shem-Tov

Jacob's Courage. Romance and Survival Amidst the Horrors of War,
by Charles S. Weinblatt

Want to be an AP book reviewer?

Reviews are very important in a world dominated by the social media and social proof. Please drop us a line if you want to join the *AP review team* and show us at least one review already posted on Amazon for one of our books. info@amsterdampublishers.com

www.ingramcontent.com/pod-product-compliance
Lightning Source LLC
Chambersburg PA
CBHW020724150726
48196CB00028B/819/J